Track Diagrams — England South and

C000265153

These diagrams cover the lines of British Rail's former Southern Region together w[ith]   [...]rial layouts. It is, in general, up-to-date to 1st October 1994.

Mileages often vary slightly between different official records, but, in general, th[e ...] [h]ave been used. Station mileages are taken from the mid-point of the platforms, or, in [...]

British Rail lines are electrified (usually 3rd rail) except where otherwise noted, likewise London Underground lines are 4th rail.

These diagrams have been compiled substantially from information supplied from various British Rail Sources up to 31 March 1994 with some subsequent updates, supplemented by other data and amended from observations. In some cases distinctions between BR ownership and other parties are not shown and no inferences concerning ownership should therefore be drawn.

The assistance of numerous BR and London Underground officials is gratefully acknowledged. Other acknowledgements are due to members of the Branch Line Society, the London Underground Railway Society, the Railway Correspondence and Travel Society, other railway societies, Malcolm Malins and also representatives of the other private and preserved systems featured.

Cartographer: John Yonge   Consultant editor: Gerald Jacobs

KEY

———	Running line	A 'broken' line indicates 'in situ' but out of use proposed or under construction.	
———	Siding		

——┼—— BR/LU boundary

——┆—— Signal box/centre area limits
CX │ D
SB │ SC

⌐--⌐ Tunnel

=== Viaduct

Selected Motorway & Trunk Road bridges over rail

——┼—— Level Crossing (signalled)

——┆—— Crossing (telephone)

←——→ Track signalled in both directions (a double arrow indicates normal direction of travel)

——⌐— Limit of conductor rail

——⌿— Private siding boundary, often marked by a gate

—⊖— Turntable

〜〜〜 Wall/Bank

93 Whole mileposts, shown on the appropriate side of the line (for BR, etc)

32 Whole kilometre posts (for London Underground & Eurotunnel) usually on the appropriate side of the line

81.3 End of mileage run.

3 Platform with number

⊏⊐ Provisional proposed platform

▭ Platform out of use

⊠ (P) Signal box with code

⊠ Gate box

▫ Ground frame

○ Water Tower

∧ Summit

• Location spot

86.34 Distance in miles and chains (80 chains to 1 mile; 22 yards — about 20 metres — equal 1 chain)

86·34 Distance in Kilometres. (Eurotunnel, London Underground and Docklands Light Railway)

BML ELR (Engineers Line Reference)

LONDON UNDERGROUND SIGNALLING

LU signalling is controlled at some places by local Signal Cabins, or for a long part or the whole of some lines by Signal Control Centres.

Because of different cables, LU has Interlocking Machines operated by air motors (or comparable equipment) in unmanned rooms near points, except where a local cabin has an interlocking lever frame. IMR's (and equivalent rooms) are included in these maps, but purely Relay Rooms (and their equivalents) are not. IMR's bear the name of the adjacent station unless otherwise noted: (e) indicates location at the end of the platform, (m) in the middle of the platform.

▫ (MAA) Local Cabin or Control Centre with code(s) controlled.

(MU) Unmanned Interlocking Machine (or comparable equipment) Room with code.

(NP) Interlocking within manned cabin with code(s) controlled

(NP) Interlocking inside former cabin

▫ Ground Frame

BS │ BT Code area boundaries (where not separated by a long stretch of plain track(s)

PRICE £6.95   ISBN: 1 898319 07 3

Published by the Quail Map Company, 31 Lincoln Road, Exeter EX4 2DZ (Telephone & Fax Exeter (01392) 430277)
and printed by the Brightsea Press Ltd, Exeter.
© John Yonge, Gerald Jacobs and The Quail Map Company. October 1994

ABBREVIATIONS

AA	Acid application
ABCL	Automatic Barrier Crossing (Locally Monitored)
AHB	Automatic Half Barriers
AOCL	Automatic Open Crossing – (Locally Monitored)
ARR	Arrival
bdy	boundary
BCH	Branch
BR	British Rail
CCTV	Closed circuit television
CE	Civil Engineer
CET	Controlled Emission Toilet Discharge
CM & EE	Cheif Mechanical & Electrical Engineer
COM	Change of mileage
CR	Cripple siding
CW	Carriage washer
DEP	Departure
DISC	Connections disconnected
DN	Down
DPL	Down Passenger Loop
E	East
e	electrified
EB	Eastbound
EMU	Electric multiple-unit
ET	Eurotunnel
FA	Flushing apron
FP	Fuelling point (or Footpath)
GB	Gate Box
GC	former Great Central Railway
GDS	Goods
GE	former Great Eastern Railway
GF	Ground frame
GN	former Great Northern Railway
GW	former Great Western Railway
H	Headshunt
HH	Hopper House
IECC	Integrated Electronic Control Centre
Jn	Junction
Jt	Joint
km	Kilometres
L	Wheel lathe
LBSC	former London, Brighton & South Coast Railway
LC	Level Crossing
LCD	former London, Chatham and Dover Railway
LGV	Ligne à Grande Vitesse (High Speed line)
LHS	Loco. Holding Siding
LM	London Midland
LNE	former London & North Eastern Railway
LNW	former London & North Western Railway
LP	Loop
LPG	Liquified Petroleum Gas
LPTB	former London Passenger Transport Board
LS	Locomotive shed

LSW	former London and South Western Railway
LU	London Underground Ltd.
LW	Locomotive washer
M	Middle
M & EE	Mechanical & Electrical Engineer
MN	Main
MSW	former Midland & South Western Jn Railway
N	North
n	Not electrified
NB	Northbound
NIRU	Not in regular use
N & SW Jn	former North & South Western Junction Rly
O/H	Overhead
OOU	Out of use
Open	Open Crossing – no lights
P	Points padlocked
PAD	Prefabricated Assembly Depot
PS	Private siding
PSB	Power signal box
PW	Permanent Way
REC	Reception
REV	Reversible
RFD	Railfreight Distribution
R/G	Miniature red/green warning lights
RR	Run-round
S	South
SB	Signal box or Southbound
SC	Signalling Centre
S&C	Switches & Crossings
Sdg(s)	Siding(s)
SD	Sand drag
SE	former South Eastern Railway
SF	Shunting frame
SN	Shunting neck
SNCF	Société Nationale des Chemins de Fer Français (French National Rlys)
SO	former Southern Railway (1923-47)
SP	Switch Panel
S & T	Signal & Telegraph
T	Tamper
TGV	Train à Grande Vitesse (High Speed Train)
TLF	Trainload Freight
TMD	Traction Maintenance Depot
TMO	Trainmen operated
TPO	Travelling Post Office
T&RSMD	Traction & Rolling Stock Maintenance Depot
UH	Unloading Hopper
UKAEA	United Kingdom Atomic Energy Authority
UPL	Up Passenger Loop
V or Vdct	Viaduct
W	West
WB	Weighbridge or westbound
WL	former West London Joint Railway
WLE	former West London Extension Joint Railway
yds	yards

In the same series:
1 Scotland (1993) £5.00
2 England East & Anglia (out of print, new edition proposed 1995)
3 Western Region (out of print)
4 London Midland Region (out of print)
The Quail Map Company produces and imports railway maps of various countries and cities. A catalogue will be sent on request.

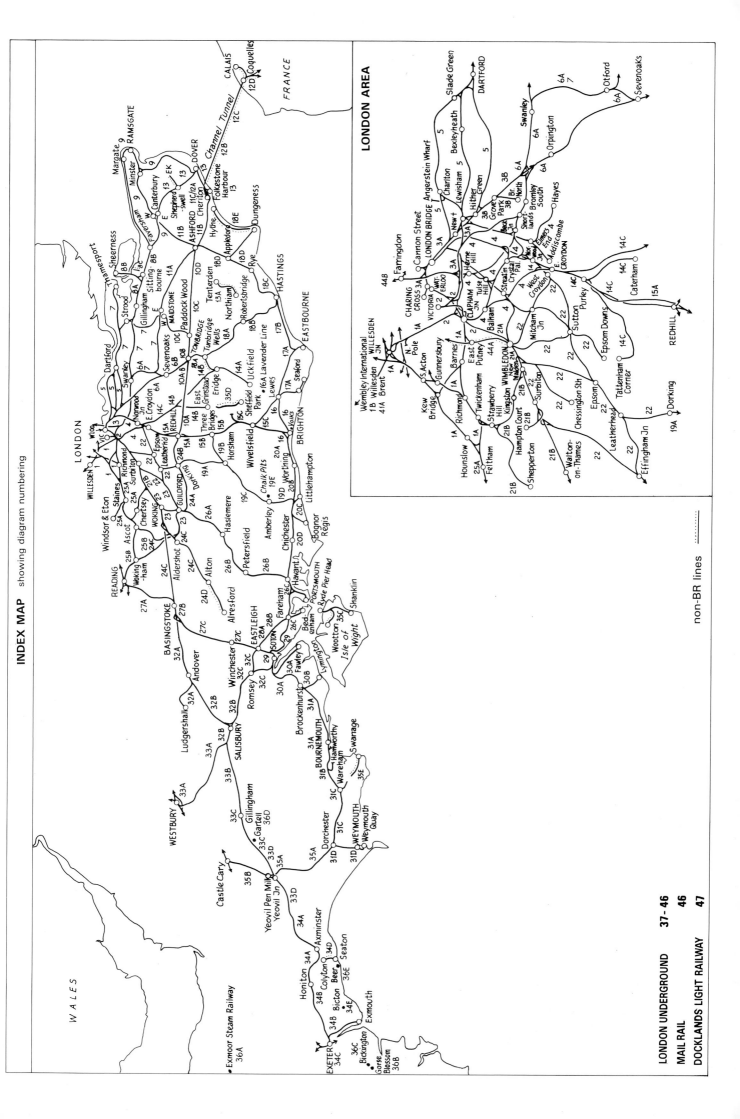

INDEX MAP showing diagram numbering

LONDON AREA

LONDON UNDERGROUND 37 - 46

MAIL RAIL 46

DOCKLANDS LIGHT RAILWAY 47

non-BR lines

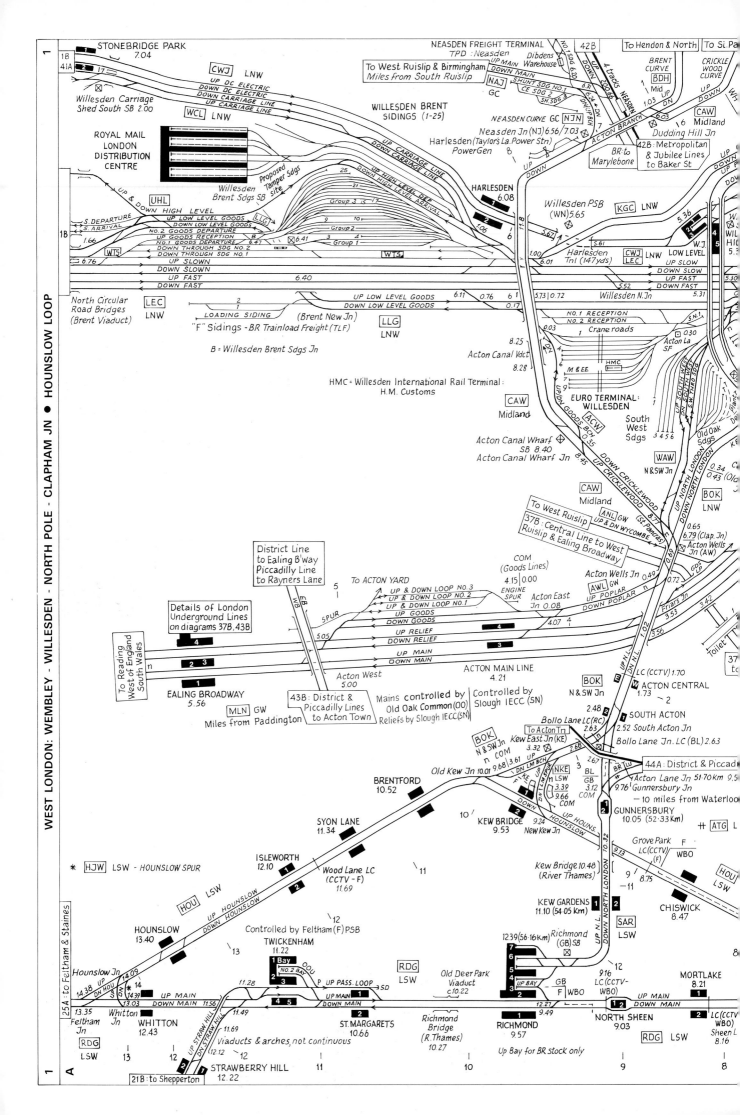

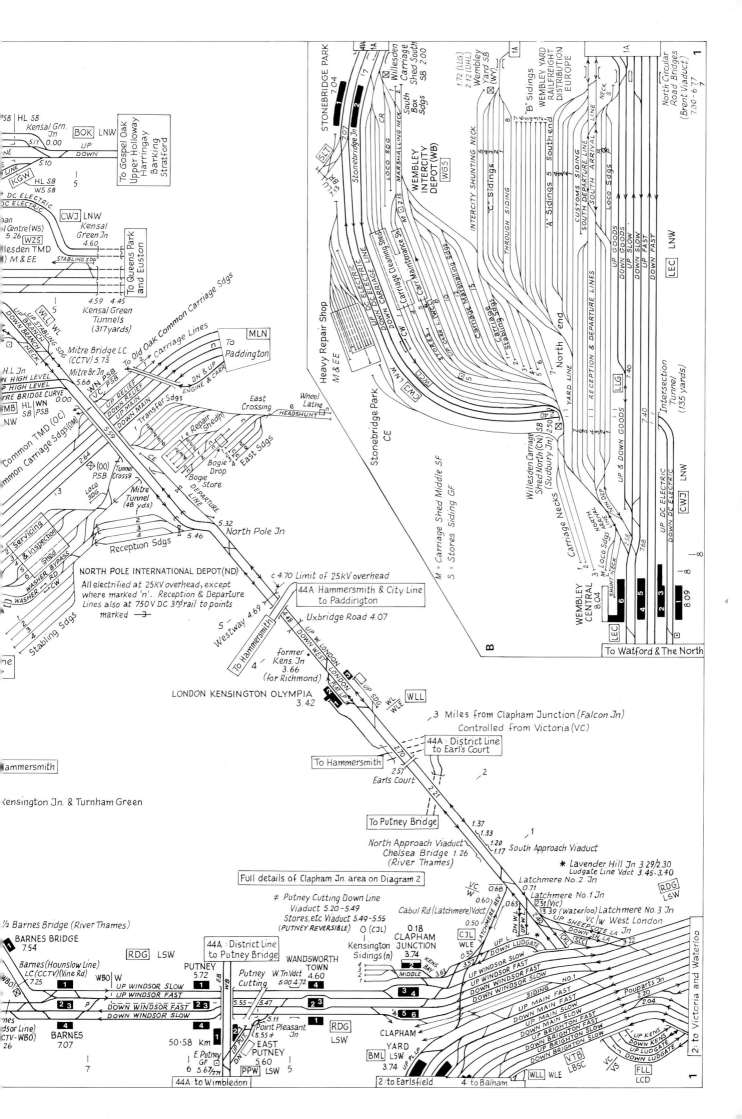

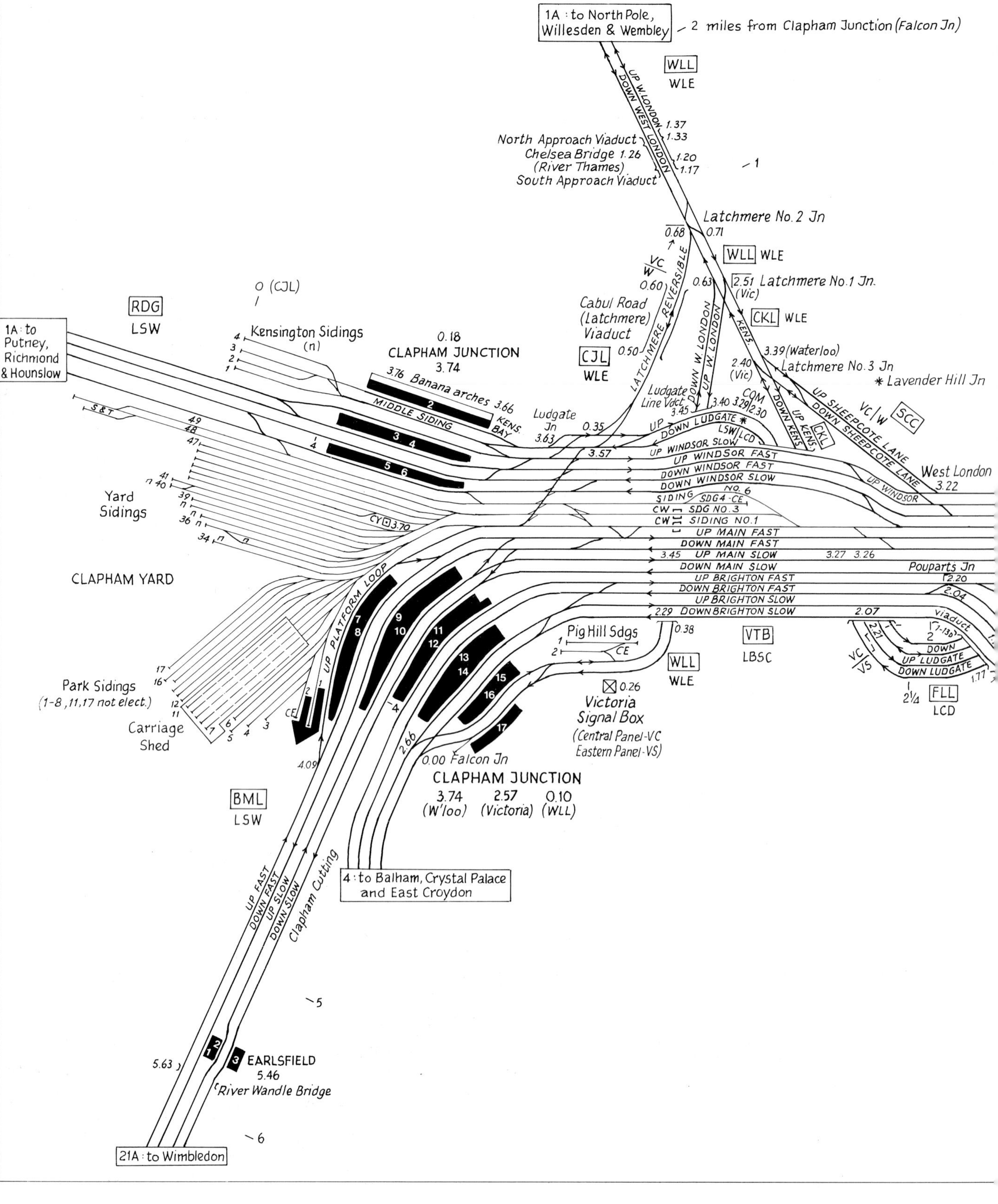

1A : to North Pole,
Willesden & Wembley — 2 miles from Clapham Junction (Falcon Jn)

WLL
WLE

UP W LONDON
DOWN WEST LONDON

1.37
1.33
North Approach Viaduct
Chelsea Bridge 1.26
(River Thames)
South Approach Viaduct
1.20
1.17

~1

Latchmere No. 2 Jn

0.68
0.71

WLL WLE

VC
W
0.60

0.63

2.51 Latchmere No.1 Jn.
(Vic)

CKL WLE

LATCHMERE REVERSIBLE

UP W LONDON
DOWN W LONDON

UP KENS
DOWN KENS

UP SHEEPCOTE LANE
DOWN SHEEPCOTE LANE

3.39 (Waterloo)
Latchmere No. 3 Jn

* Lavender Hill Jn

Cabul Road
(Latchmere)
Viaduct

CJL
WLE

0.50

2.40
(Vic)

COM
3.29
2.30

VC/W

SCC

RDG
LSW

0 (CJL)

Kensington Sidings
(n)

0.18
CLAPHAM JUNCTION
3.74

1A : to Putney,
Richmond
& Hounslow

4
3
2
1

3.76 Banana arches 3.66

MIDDLE SIDING

2

KENS.
BAY

Ludgate
Jn
3.63

0.35

Ludgate
Line Vidct
3.45

3.40

CKL

West London
3.22

S & T

4.9
4.8
4.7

3 4

1 4

5 6

UP LUDGATE
DOWN LUDGATE
LSW/LCD

3.57

UP WINDSOR SLOW
UP WINDSOR FAST
DOWN WINDSOR FAST
DOWN WINDSOR SLOW

NO. 6
SIDING SDG 4 -CE
CW SDG NO. 3
CW SIDING NO.1

UP WINDSOR

Yard
Sidings

4.1
40

3.9

36

34

n

n

n

n

CY 3.70

UP MAIN FAST
DOWN MAIN FAST
3.45 UP MAIN SLOW
DOWN MAIN SLOW
UP BRIGHTON FAST
DOWN BRIGHTON FAST
UP BRIGHTON SLOW
2.29 DOWN BRIGHTON SLOW

3.27 3.26

Pouparts Jn

2.20

2.04

2.07

CLAPHAM YARD

UP PLATFORM LOOP

7
8

9
10

11
12

13
14

15
16

17

Pig Hill Sdgs
1
2

CE

0.38

WLL
WLE

VTB
LBSC

Viaduct

7.13b

2
1

VC
VS

UP LUDGATE
DOWN
DOWN LUDGATE

1.77

Park Sidings
(1-8, 11, 17 not elect.)

17
16

12
11

1

CE

1

1

6
5

5
4

3

4

0.26

Victoria
Signal Box

(Central Panel-VC
Eastern Panel-VS)

1
2¼
FLL
LCD

Carriage
Shed

BML
LSW

4.09

2.66

2.57

0.00 Falcon Jn

CLAPHAM JUNCTION

3.74
(W'loo)

2.57
(Victoria)

0.10
(WLL)

UP FAST
DOWN FAST
UP SLOW
DOWN SLOW

Clapham Cutting

4 : to Balham, Crystal Palace
and East Croydon

~5

5.63

1 2

3

EARLSFIELD
5.46
River Wandle Bridge

~6

21A : to Wimbledon

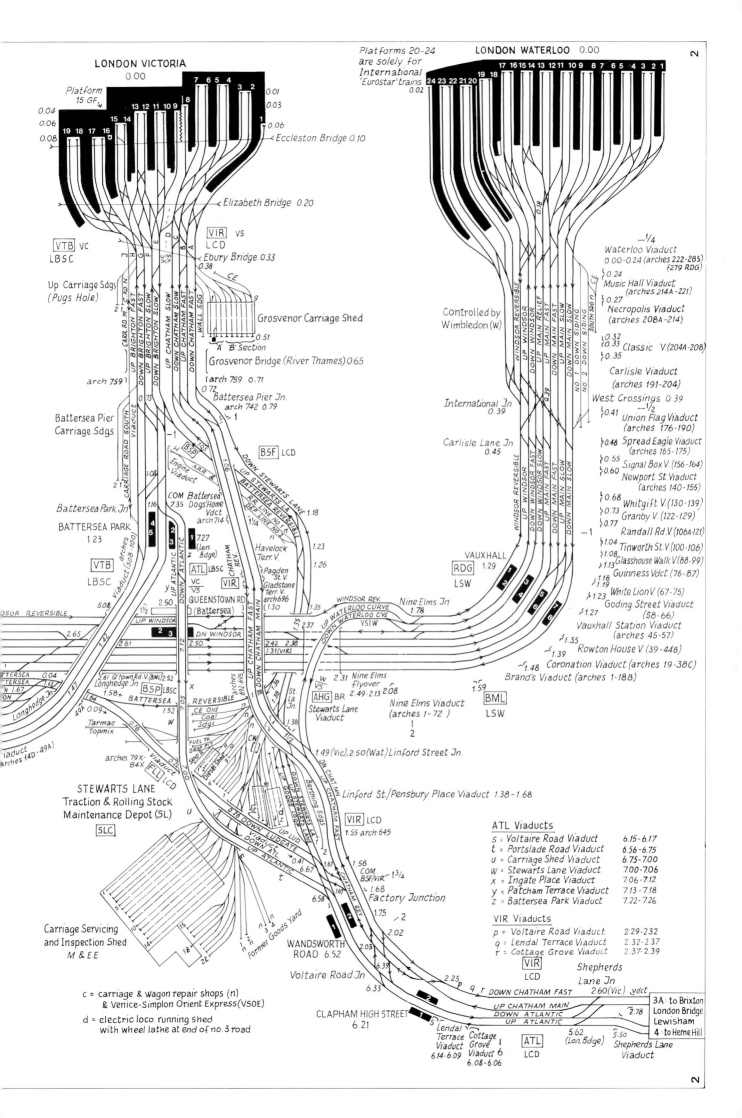

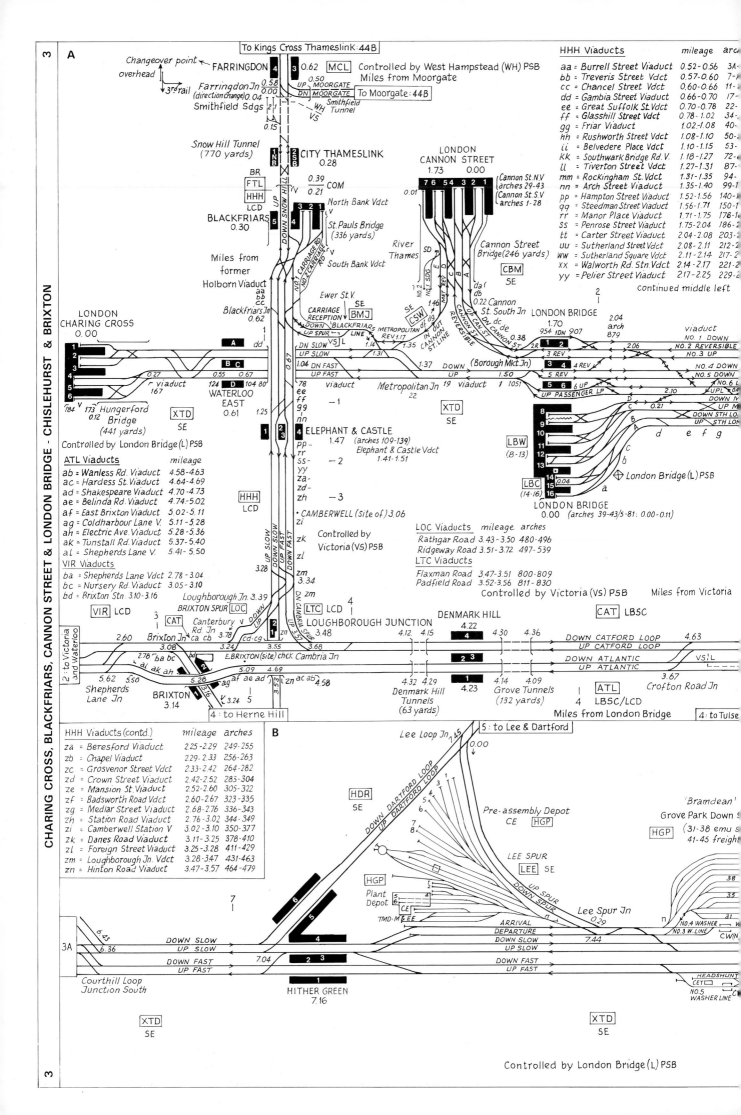

To Kings Cross Thameslink : 44B

Changeover point overhead
3rd rail

FARRINGDON 4 3 0.62 MCL Controlled by West Hampstead (WH) PSB
Miles from Moorgate

0.58 UP MOORGATE 0.50
Farringdon Jn 0.00
(direction change) 0.04 DN MOORGATE

Smithfield Sdgs 2 WH To Moorgate : 44B
VS Smithfield Tunnel
0.15

Snow Hill Tunnel (770 yards)

1 NB 2 SB CITY THAMESLINK 0.28

BR
FTL
HHH LCD

0.39 COM
0.21

North Bank Vdct

BLACKFRIARS 0.30 5 4 3 2 1

St.Pauls Bridge (336 yards)

LONDON CANNON STREET 1.73 0.00
7 6 5 4 3 2 1 Cannon St.N.V arches 29-43
Cannon St.S.V arches 1-28

South Bank Vdct

Miles from former Holborn Viaduct
aa
bb
cc

Ewer St.V.
CARRIAGE RECEPTION SE BMJ
DOWN BLACKFRIARS LINE

Blackfriars Jn 0.62

River Thames

Cannon Street Bridge (246 yards) CBM SE

CSW SE
METROPOLITAN REV 1.17

LONDON BRIDGE 1.70

2.04 arch 879 viaduct NO.1 DOWN

LONDON CHARING CROSS 0.00

ATL Viaducts mileage
ab = Wanless Rd. Viaduct 4.58-4.63
ac = Hardess St. Viaduct 4.64-4.69
ad = Shakespeare Viaduct 4.70-4.73
ae = Belinda Rd. Viaduct 4.74-5.02
af = East Brixton Viaduct 5.02-5.11
ag = Coldharbour Lane V. 5.11-5.28
ah = Electric Ave. Viaduct 5.28-5.36
ak = Tunstall Rd. Viaduct 5.37-5.40
al = Shepherds Lane V. 5.41-5.50

VIR Viaducts
ba = Shepherds Lane Vdct 2.78-3.04
bc = Nursery Rd. Viaduct 3.05-3.10
bd = Brixton Stn. 3.10-3.16

VIR LCD CAT

Brixton Jn 2.60
3.08 3.78
Canterbury Rd. Jn
2.78 ba bc

Shepherds Lane Jn 5.62 5.50

BRIXTON 3.14

4 : to Herne Hill

Controlled by London Bridge (L) PSB

HHH Viaducts	mileage	arc
aa = Burrell Street Viaduct	0.52-0.56	3A
bb = Treveris Street Vdct	0.57-0.60	7
cc = Chancel Street Vdct	0.60-0.66	11
dd = Gambia Street Viaduct	0.66-0.70	17
ee = Great Suffolk St.Vdct	0.70-0.78	22
ff = Glasshill Street Vdct	0.78-1.02	34
gg = Friar Viaduct	1.02-1.08	40
hh = Rushworth Street Vdct	1.08-1.10	50
ii = Belvedere Place Vdct	1.10-1.15	53
kk = Southwark Bridge Rd. V.	1.18-1.27	72
ll = Tiverton Street Vdct	1.27-1.31	87
mm = Rockingham St. Vdct	1.31-1.35	94
nn = Arch Street Viaduct	1.35-1.40	99
pp = Hampton Street Viaduct	1.52-1.56	140
qq = Steedman Street Viaduct	1.56-1.71	150
rr = Manor Place Viaduct	1.71-1.75	178
ss = Penrose Street Viaduct	1.75-2.04	186
tt = Carter Street Viaduct	2.04-2.08	203
uu = Sutherland Street Vdct	2.08-2.11	212
ww = Sutherland Square Vdct	2.11-2.14	217
xx = Walworth Rd. Stn. Vdct	2.14-2.17	221
yy = Pelier Street Viaduct	2.17-2.25	229

continued middle left

ELEPHANT & CASTLE 1.47 (arches 109-139)
Elephant & Castle Vdct 1.41-1.51

HHH LCD

Controlled by Victoria (VS) PSB

LOC Viaducts mileage arches
Rathgar Road 3.43-3.50 480-496
Ridgeway Road 3.51-3.72 497-539

LTC Viaducts
Flaxman Road 3.47-3.51 800-809
Padfield Road 3.52-3.56 811-830

Controlled by Victoria (VS) PSB Miles from Victoria

DENMARK HILL 4.22 CAT LBSC

LOUGHBOROUGH JUNCTION 3.48

DOWN CATFORD LOOP 4.63
UP CATFORD LOOP

DOWN ATLANTIC VS L
UP ATLANTIC

3.67 Crofton Road Jn

Denmark Hill Tunnels (63 yards) Grove Tunnels (132 yards)

ATL LBSC/LCD Miles from London Bridge 4 : to Tulse

LONDON BRIDGE 0.00 (arches 39-43/5-81: 0.00-0.11)

LBW (8-13) LBC (14-16)

London Bridge (L) PSB

XTD SE

HHH Viaducts (contd.)	mileage	arches
za = Beresford Viaduct	2.25-2.29	249-255
zb = Chapel Viaduct	2.29-2.33	256-263
zc = Grosvenor Street Vdct	2.33-2.42	264-282
zd = Crown Street Viaduct	2.42-2.52	283-304
ze = Mansion St. Viaduct	2.52-2.60	305-322
zf = Badsworth Road Vdct	2.60-2.67	323-335
zg = Medlar Street Viaduct	2.68-2.76	336-343
zh = Station Road Viaduct	2.76-3.02	344-349
zi = Camberwell Station V.	3.02-3.10	350-377
zk = Danes Road Viaduct	3.11-3.25	378-410
zl = Foreign Street Viaduct	3.25-3.28	411-429
zm = Loughborough Jn. Vdct	3.28-3.47	431-463
zn = Hinton Road Viaduct	3.47-3.57	464-479

B

5 : to Lee & Dartford

Lee Loop Jn 7.45
0.00

DOWN DARTFORD LOOP
UP DARTFORD LOOP

HDR SE

Pre-assembly Depot CE HGP

'Bramdean'
Grove Park Down S
(31-38 emu s
41-45 freight
HGP

LEE SPUR LEE SE

HGP Plant Depot CE

Lee Spur Jn 0.29

TMD-M EE

NO.4 WASHER W
NO.3 W.LINE
CW(N

ARRIVAL
DEPARTURE
DOWN SLOW 7.44
UP SLOW

DOWN SLOW
UP SLOW

Courthill Loop Junction South

DOWN FAST 7.04
UP FAST

DOWN FAST
UP FAST

HITHER GREEN 7.16

HEADSHUNT CET
NO.5 WASHER LINE

XTD SE

XTD SE

Controlled by London Bridge (L) PSB

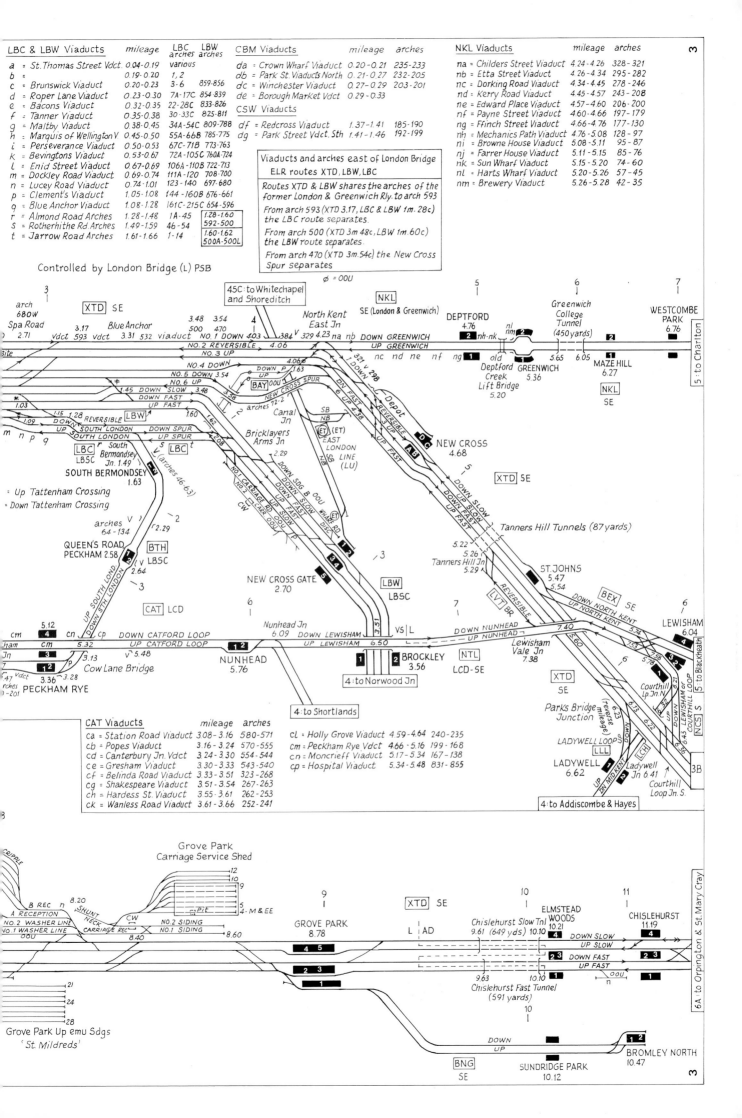

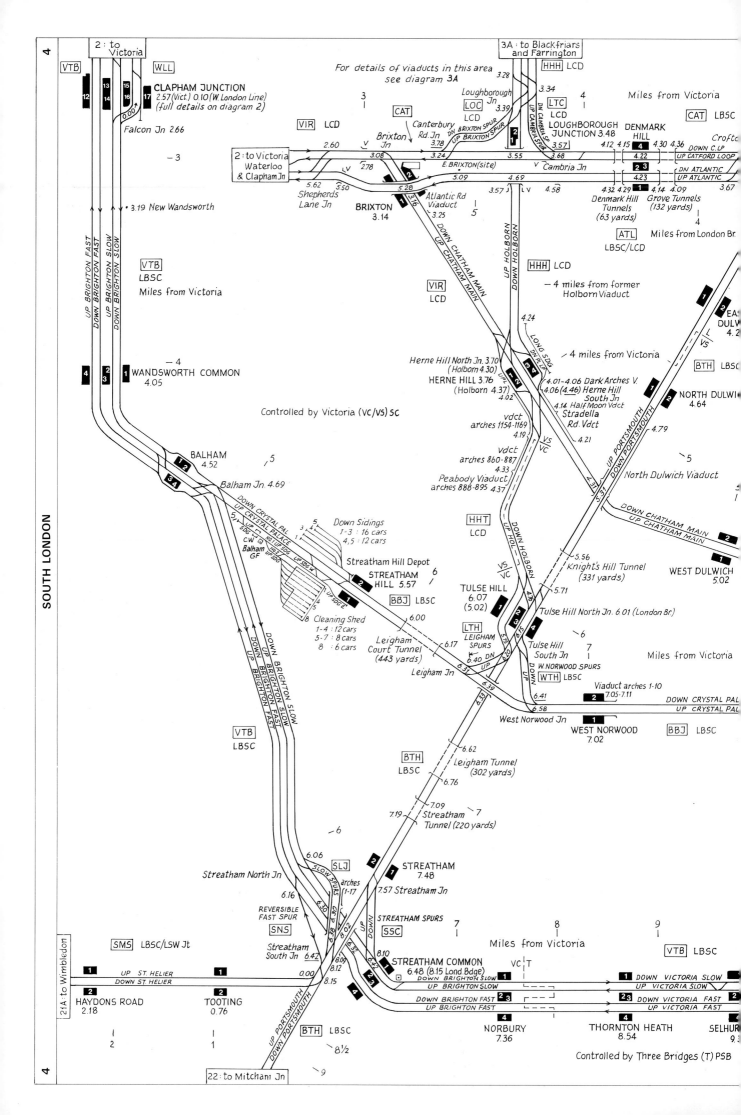

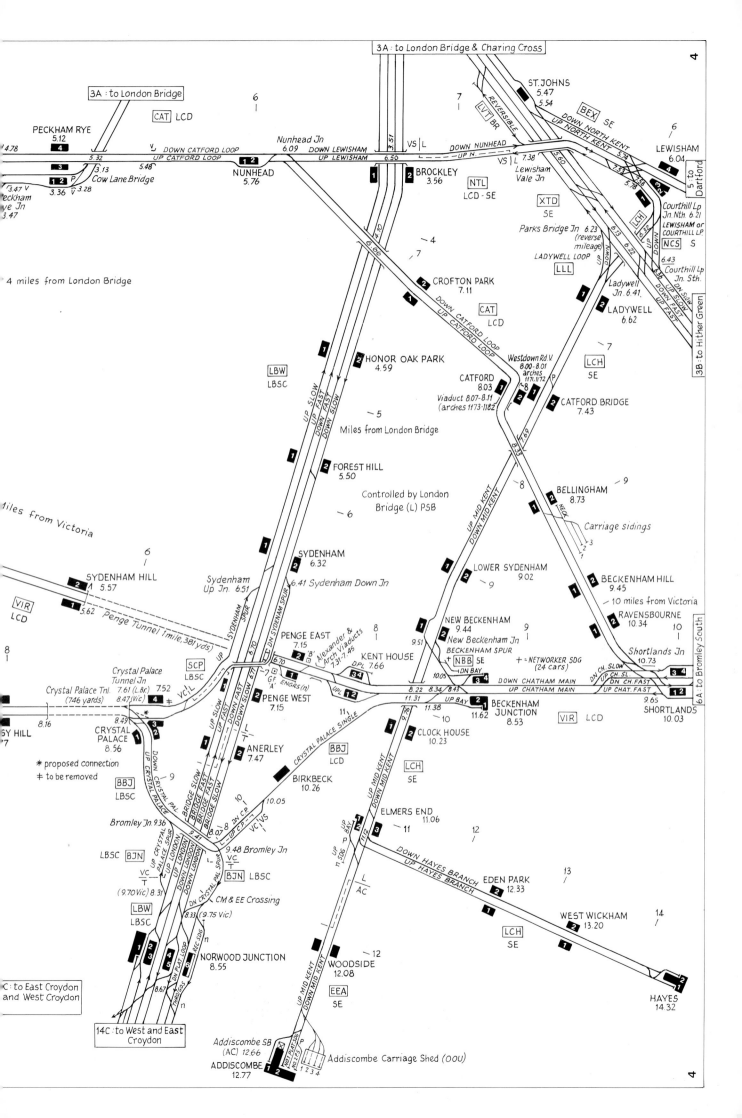

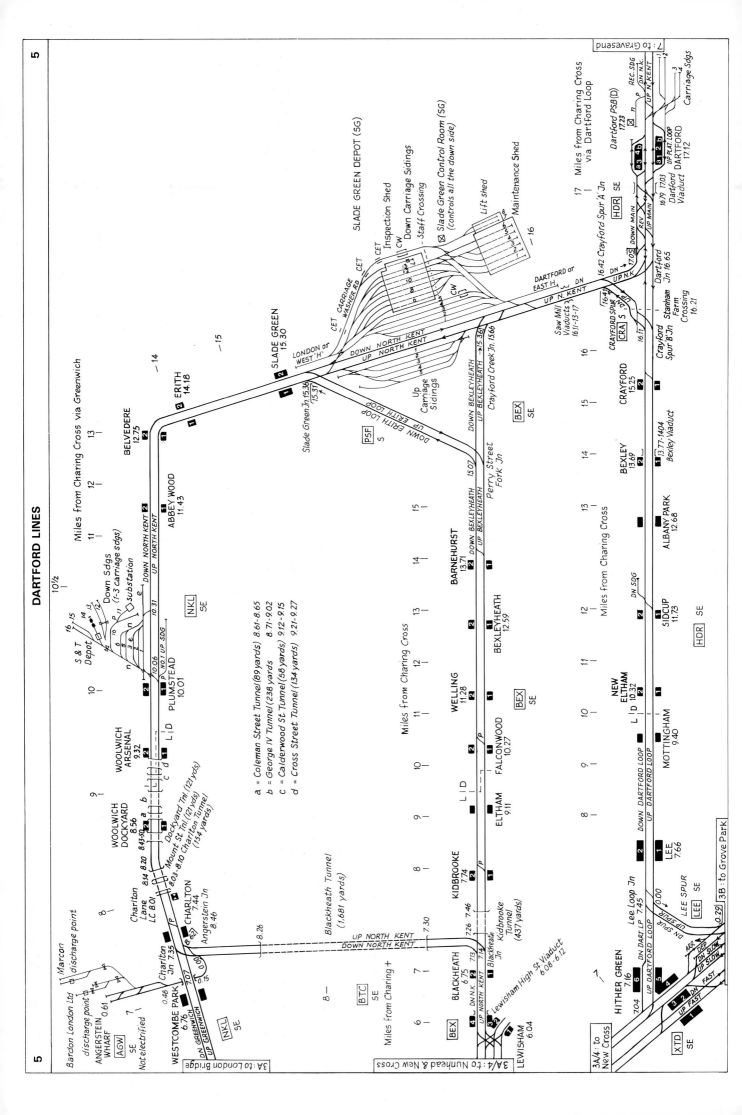

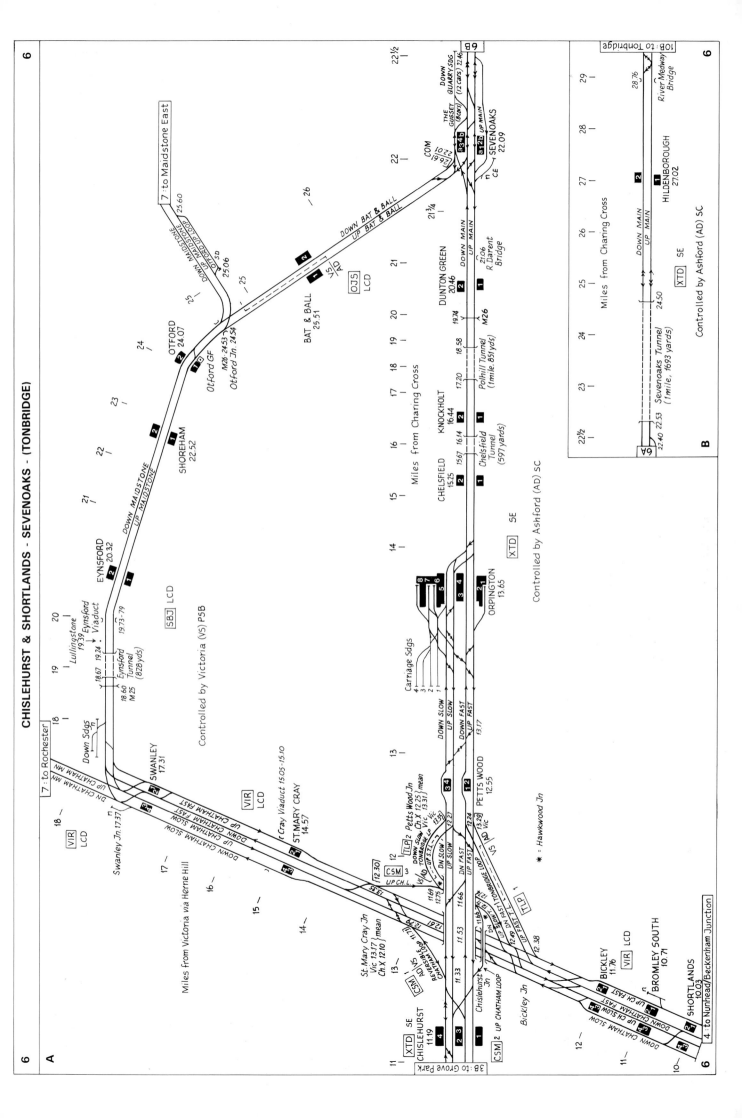

CHISLEHURST & SHORTLANDS - SEVENOAKS - (TONBRIDGE)

DARTFORD - STROOD - MAIDSTONE ● SWANLEY - ROCHESTER ● SWANLEY - MAIDSTONE

5: to Crayford & Slade Green

18   19   20   21

NORTHFLEET NEW WORK
Blue Circle Cement
LC No.3

Dartford PSB (D)
17.23

REC SDG

STONE
CROSSING
19.07
LC
1913

GREENHITHE
19.69
20.03-15

Blue Circle
η OOU

Swanscombe Sdg
GF 'K'
20.70

NORTHFLEET
21.69

Cement
loading
silo
Gypsum
intake
Tunnel
No.3

DOWN NORTH KENT   17.70   DOWN MAIN
UP NORTH KENT   UP MAIN

3 4
1 2   UP PLAT. LP

DARTFORD
17.12

*Dartford Tunnel
Bridge*

Carriage Sdgs

1
2

3
4

Stone
Crossing
(Dartford)
(ST) SB
19.14

*Greenhithe
Tunnel
(253 yards)*

DISC

SWANSCOMBE
21.14

P   P

DISC   DISC No.1   REC   GF CR
No.2 RECEPTION
DEPARTURE
GF 'A'
Maintenance Sdgs

LC No.1
(open)
Northfleet
Blue Circle
Control Room
(closed)

HDR   SE

Northfleet
22.20

6A: to St Mary Cray

18   19   20   21   22   23   24   25   26

SWANLEY
17.31   η

FARNINGHAM ROAD
20.42

LONGFIELD
23.30

MEOPHAM
25.76

3 4
1 2   17.37
Swanley
Jn

DOWN SDG η

*Farningham
Road GF
20.32*

*Darenth
Viaduct
20.68-20.74*

22.50

(Fawkham
Jn)

VS   ER

Controlled by Victoria (VS) PSB

— 18

18.67   18.60 M25
*Eynsford Tunnel
(828 yds)*
19.24

— 19

. Lullingstone

*Eynsford Vdct
19.73-19.79*

— 20

EYNSFORD
20.32   1   2

SBJ
LCD

— 21

UP MAIDSTONE   DOWN MAIDSTONE

Miles from Charing Cross via Dartford Loop

34   35   36   37   38

To Hoo Jn : see top right

DOWN →

*Stoke LC
(AOCL)
36.77*

36.79
STOKE JN
HALT (site)

Yantlet
GF

Kent Refinery
Sdg (OOU)

GRAIN
38.24
Marcroft Engng.
DOWN SDG

1
2

BP 'B' Gate
LC

Foster Yeoman LC

WB

Foster
Yeoman

38.22

Flood
gates
37.77-
38.00

Grain
Crossing
(gates)

3
4 5
6 7

Thamesport
LC

KINGSNORTH
Whitehall Sdgs
Towntrade (NIRU)

BP
Bitumen
Terminal

Pad
BP Sidings (3-7)

HTG   SE

Controlled by Dartford (D) PSB

Not electrified

Thamesport
Freightliner
Terminal

WB

Thamesport
Bulk Terminal

SHOREHAM
22.52   2

— 22

— 23

River Medway

OTFORD
24.07   1   2
Otford GF

— 24

25

26   27   28   29   30   31   32   33

Miles from Victoria via Herne Hill

M26 - 24.53
*Otford Jn
24.54*

Seal

DN PASS. LOOP
28.66

CE
η

DOWN MAIDSTONE
UP MAIDSTONE
25.06   OTFORD UP LOOP   25.60
SD   25.78

29.38   2

6A: to Sevenoaks

KEMSING
26.79

VS   ME

BOROUGH GREEN
& WROTHAM
29.46

1

SBJ   LCD

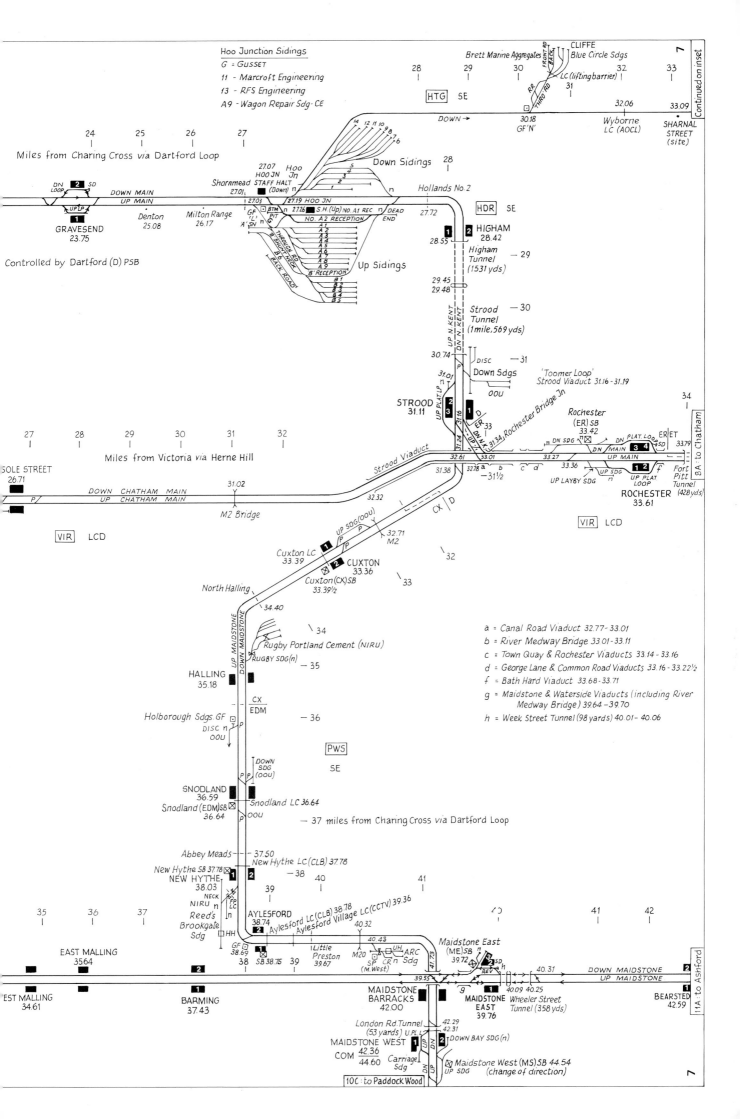

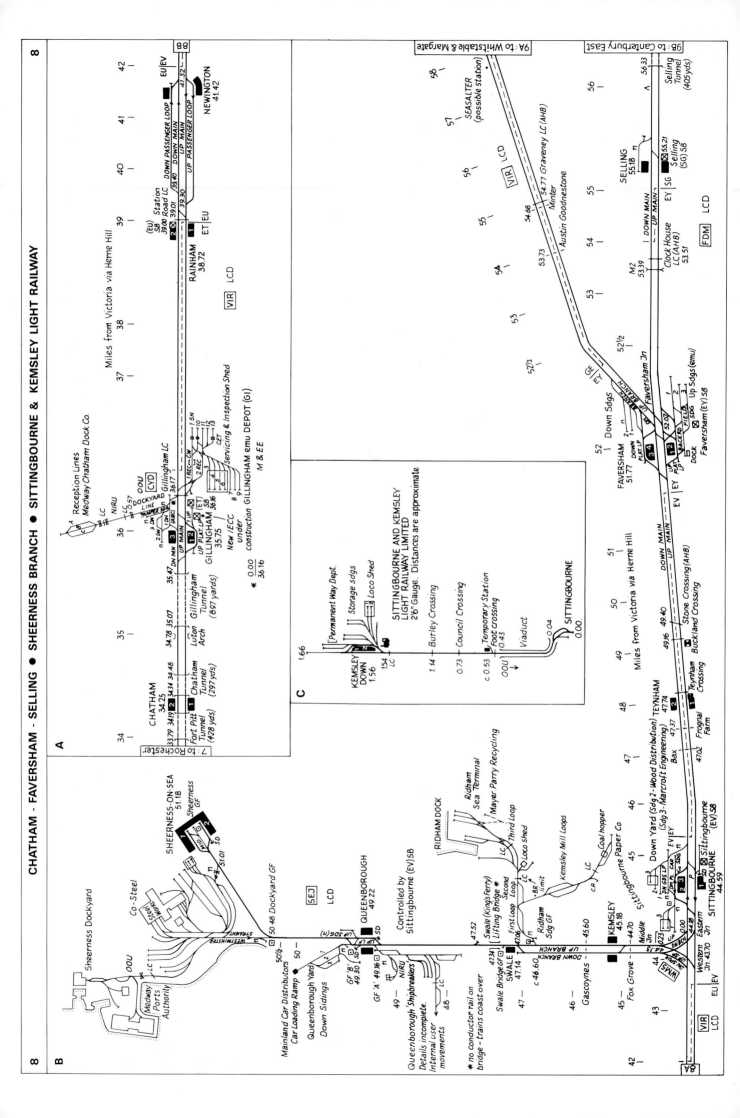

CHATHAM - FAVERSHAM - SELLING ● SHEERNESS BRANCH ● SITTINGBOURNE & KEMSLEY LIGHT RAILWAY

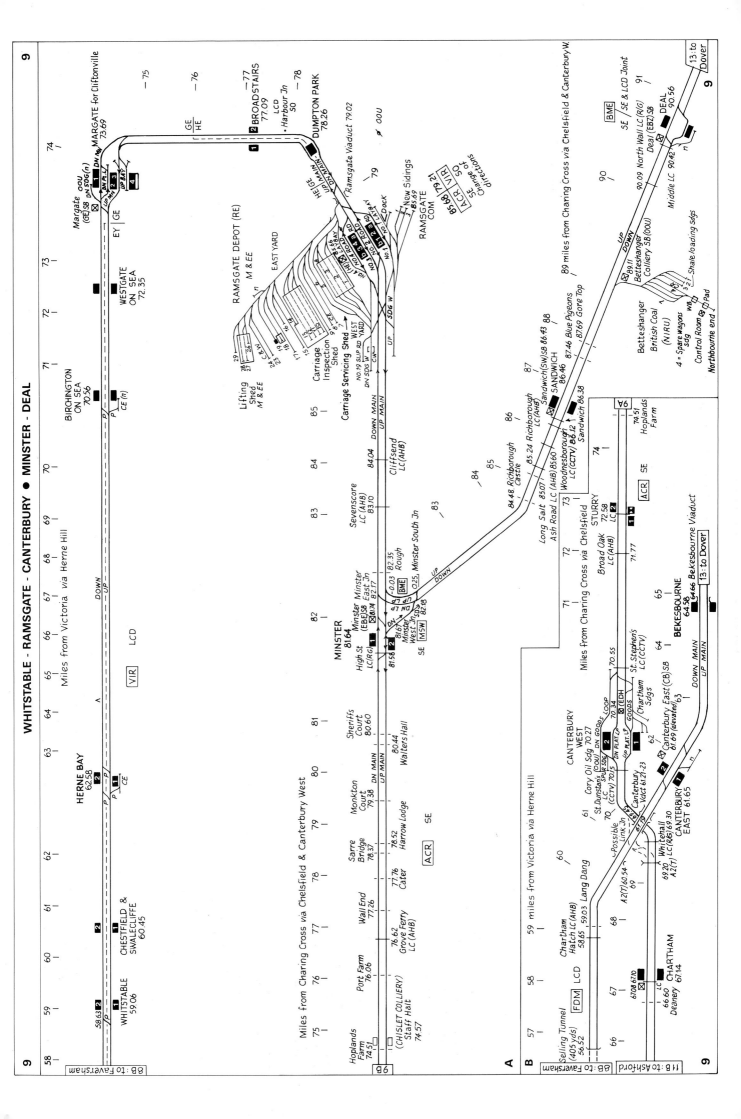

WHITSTABLE - RAMSGATE - CANTERBURY ● MINSTER ● MINSTER - DEAL

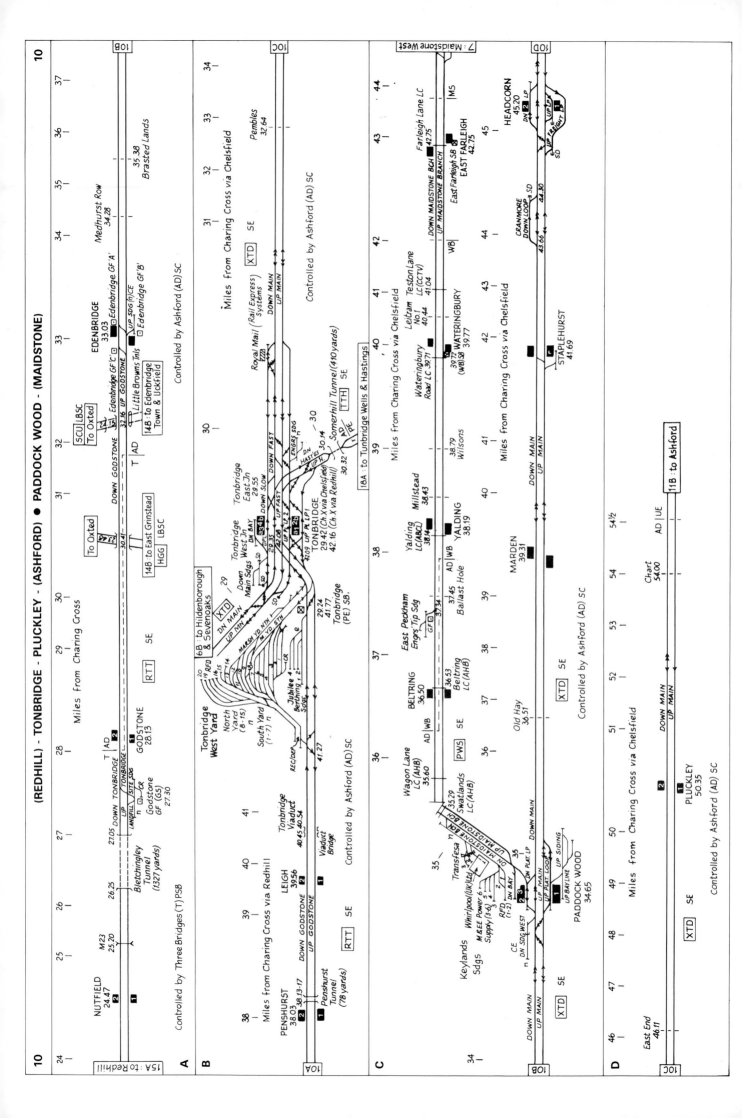

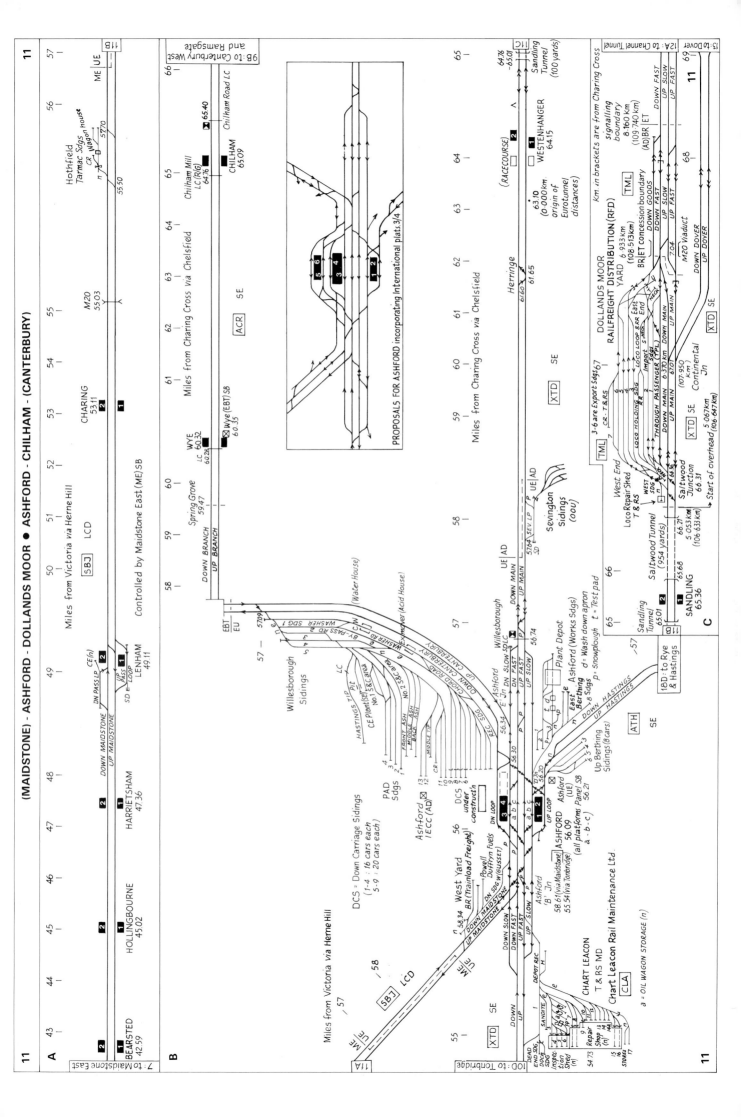

(MAIDSTONE) - ASHFORD - DOLLANDS MOOR ● ASHFORD - CHILHAM - (CANTERBURY)

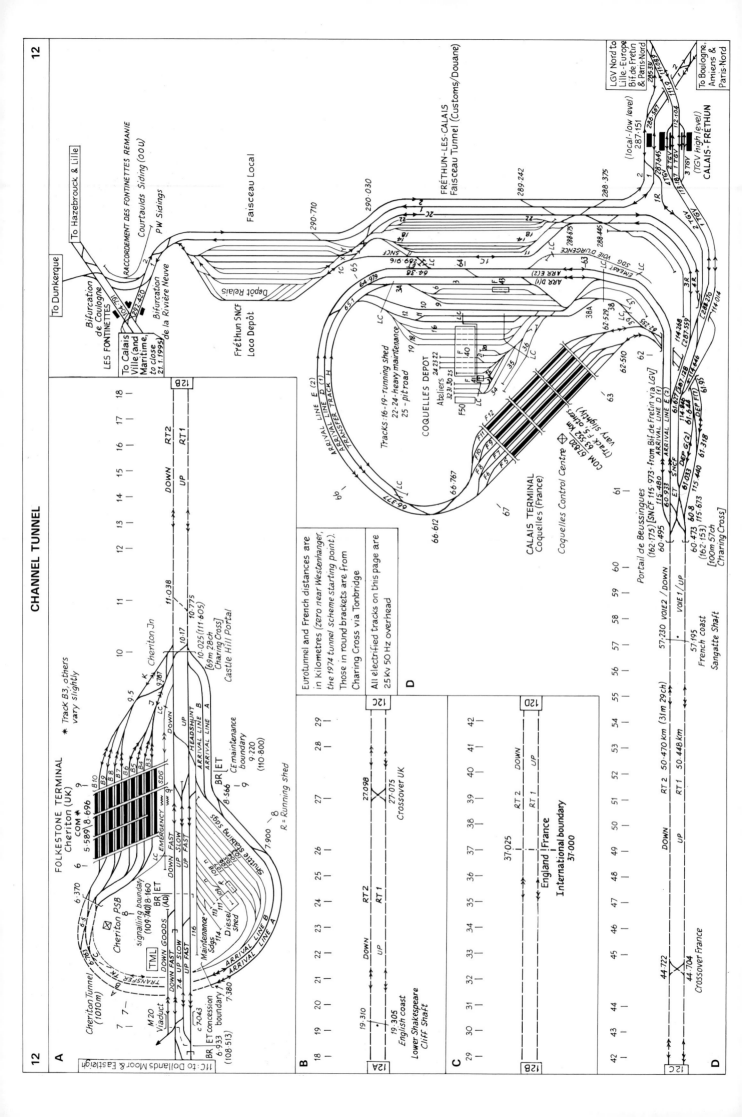

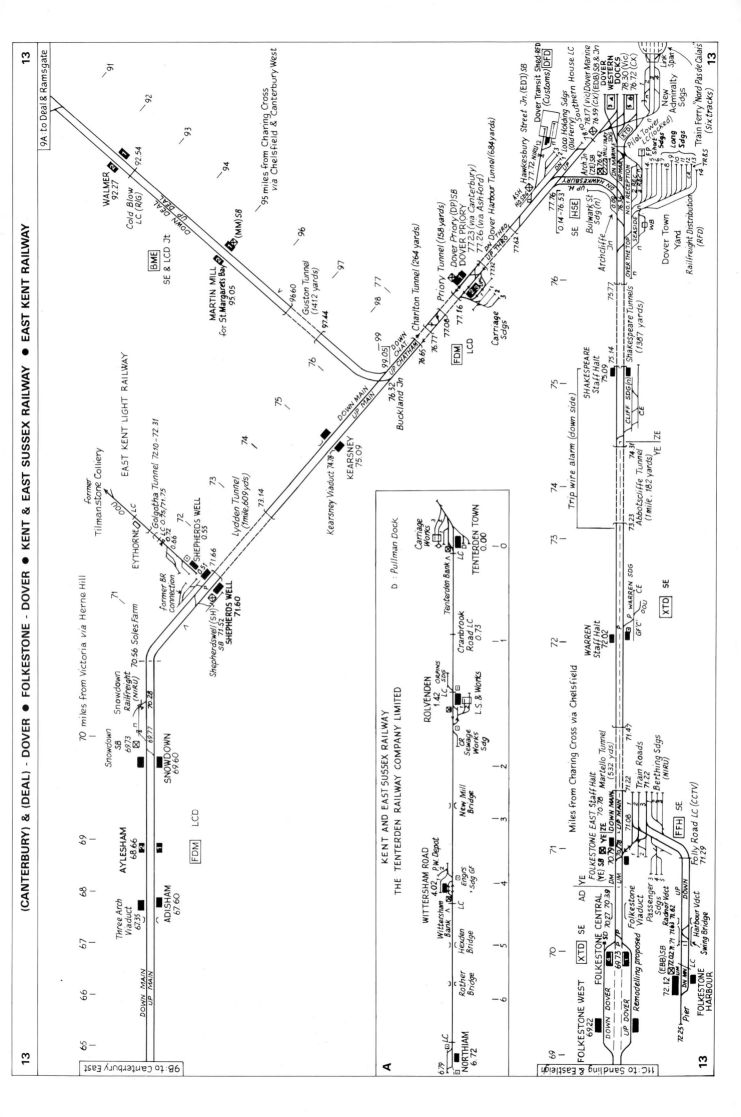

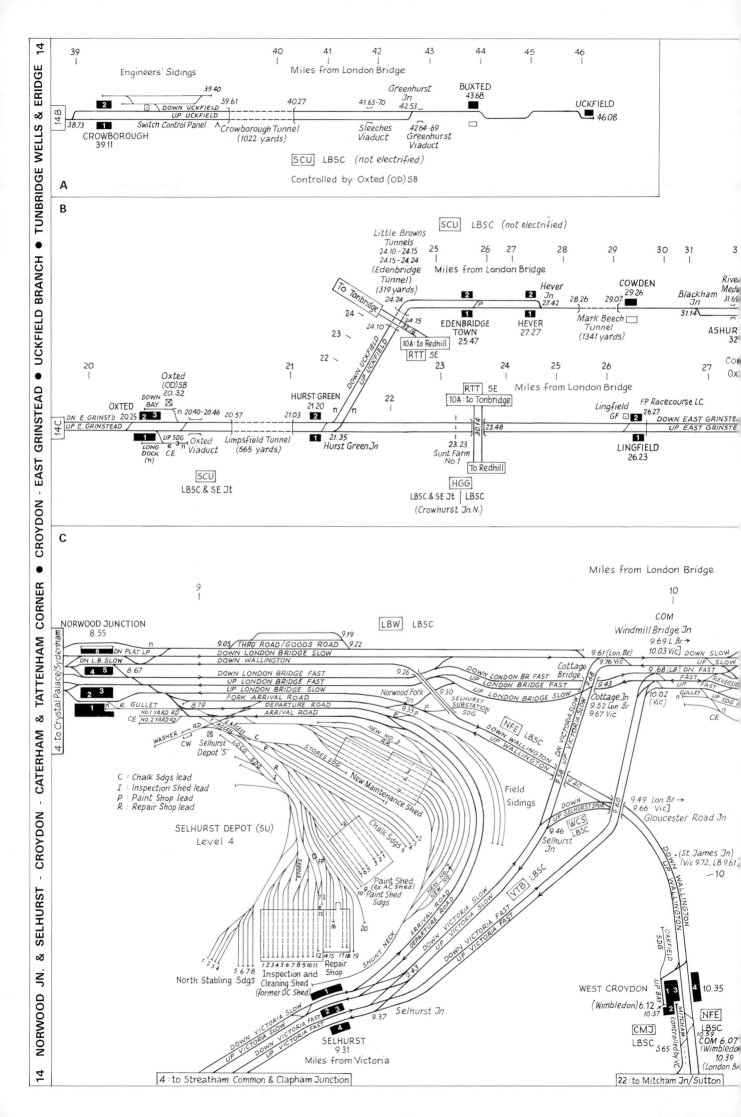

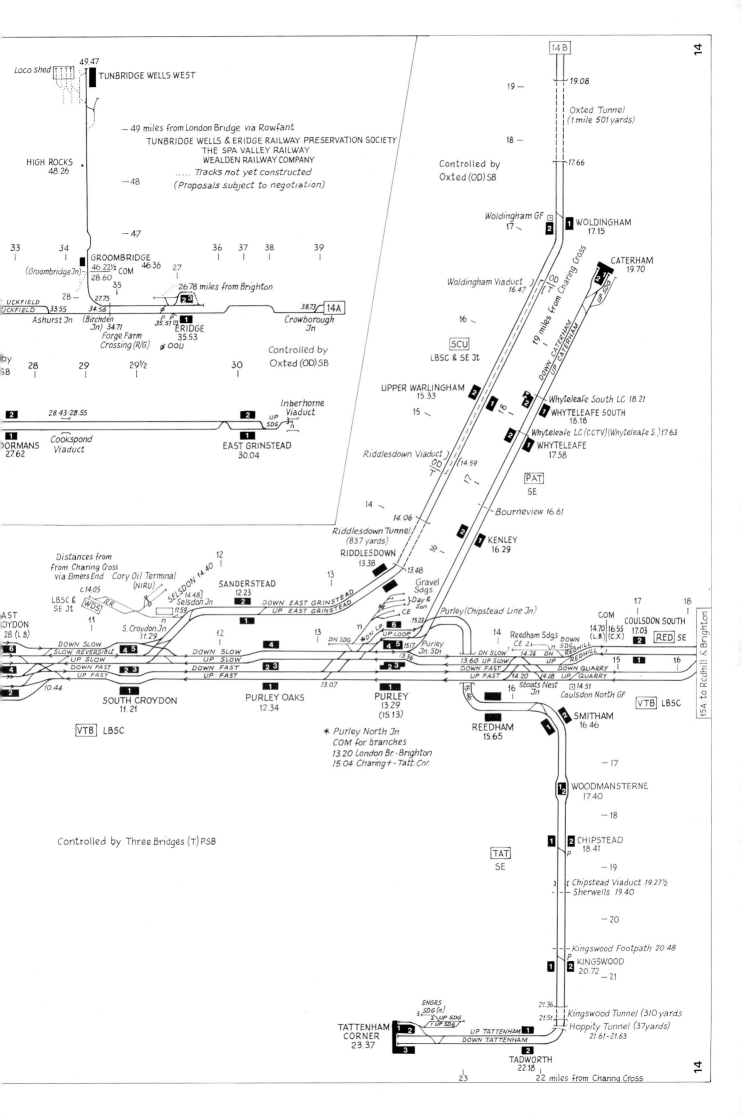

14 B

19.08

19 —

Oxted Tunnel
(1 mile 501 yards)

18 —

17.66

Controlled by
Oxted (OD) SB

Woldingham GF WOLDINGHAM
17 ⌐ **2** **1** 17.15

Loco shed 49.47
TUNBRIDGE WELLS WEST

— 49 miles from London Bridge via Rowfant
TUNBRIDGE WELLS & ERIDGE RAILWAY PRESERVATION SOCIETY
THE SPA VALLEY RAILWAY
WEALDEN RAILWAY COMPANY
..... Tracks not yet constructed
(Proposals subject to negotiation)

CATERHAM
19.70
2 1
UP SDG

HIGH ROCKS
48.26

— 48

— 47

Woldingham Viaduct
16.47

19 miles from Charing Cross

DOWN CATERHAM
UP CATERHAM

33 34 GROOMBRIDGE 36 37 38 39
46.22½ COM 46.36
(Groombridge Jn) 28.60 27
28 — 27.75 35 26.78 miles from Brighton
UCKFIELD 33.55 34.56 **2 3** 38.73 14A
UCKFIELD
Ashurst Jn (Birchden 35.51 **1** Crowborough
Jn) 34.71 P₋P ERIDGE Jn
Forge Farm 35.53
Crossing (R/G) Ø OOU

16 ⌐

SCU
LBSC & SE Jt

Controlled by
Oxted (OD) SB

UPPER WARLINGHAM **2** Whyteleafe South LC 18.21
15.33 **1** **2**
15 ⌐ **1** **WHYTELEAFE SOUTH**
18 18.18
Whyteleafe LC (CCTV) (Whyteleafe S.) 17.63
2
1 **WHYTELEAFE**
17.58

by 28 29 29½ 30
SB

2 28.43-28.55 **2** Inberhorne
Viaduct
UP
SDG
1 Cookspond **1**
DORMANS Viaduct EAST GRINSTEAD
27.62 30.04

Riddlesdown Viaduct OD
(14.59
14 ⌐
14.06
Riddlesdown Tunnel
(837 yards)
RIDDLESDOWN
13.38
13.48

PAT
SE

Bourneview 16.61

17 ⌐

16 ⌐

2 KENLEY
1 16.29

Distances from
from Charing Cross
via Elmers End Cory Oil Terminal 12
c 14.05 (NIRU) SELSDON 14.40
LBSC & WDS R.R. 14.48] SANDERSTEAD
SE Jt Selsdon Jn 12.23
11 S. Croydon Jn 11.59 **2**
AST 11.29 12 DOWN EAST GRINSTEAD 13
CROYDON **1** UP EAST GRINSTEAD
28 (L.B.) Gravel
Sdgs
Day &
Son
6 DOWN SLOW 15.23 Purley (Chipstead Line Jn)
SLOW REVERSIBLE **4 5** DOWN SLOW CE
4 UP SLOW **4** n DN LP **6**
4 DOWN FAST DN SDG UP LOOP 15.17
UP FAST 13 Purley
2 3 **2 3** 15.17 Jn Sth
2 UP FAST 13.36 13
10.44 **1** 13.07 **1**
SOUTH CROYDON PURLEY OAKS PURLEY
11.21 12.34 13.29
(15.13)

COM 17 18
COULSDON SOUTH
14.70 16.55 17.03
(L.B.) (C.X.)
2 RED SE

Reedham Sdgs DOWN
CE 2⌐ SDG REDHILL
14.24 DN
DN SLOW UP
13.60 UP SLOW REDHILL 15 **1** 16
DOWN FAST DOWN QUARRY
14.20 14.28 UP QUARRY
UP FAST DOWN QUARRY
1 16 Stoats Nest
15.40 Jn Coulsdon North GF
2 ⌂14.51
REEDHAM VTB LBSC
15.65 **1**
2 SMITHAM
16.46

VTB LBSC

* Purley North Jn
COM for branches
13.20 London Br.- Brighton
15.04 Charing + - Tatt. Cnr.

— 17

1½ WOODMANSTERNE
17.40

— 18

Controlled by Three Bridges (T) PSB

TAT
SE

1 **2** CHIPSTEAD
18.41
P

— 19

Chipstead Viaduct 19.27½
Sherwells 19.40

— 20

Kingswood Footpath 20.48
1 **2** KINGSWOOD
20.72
— 21

ENGRS
SDG (n)
3 2 UP SDG 21.36
1 UP SDG 21.51 Kingswood Tunnel (310 yards)
Hoppity Tunnel (37 yards)
TATTENHAM 21.61-21.63
CORNER **1 2** UP TATTENHAM **1**
23.37 DOWN TATTENHAM
3 **2**
TADWORTH
22.18
23 22 miles from Charing Cross

15A -to Redhill & Brighton

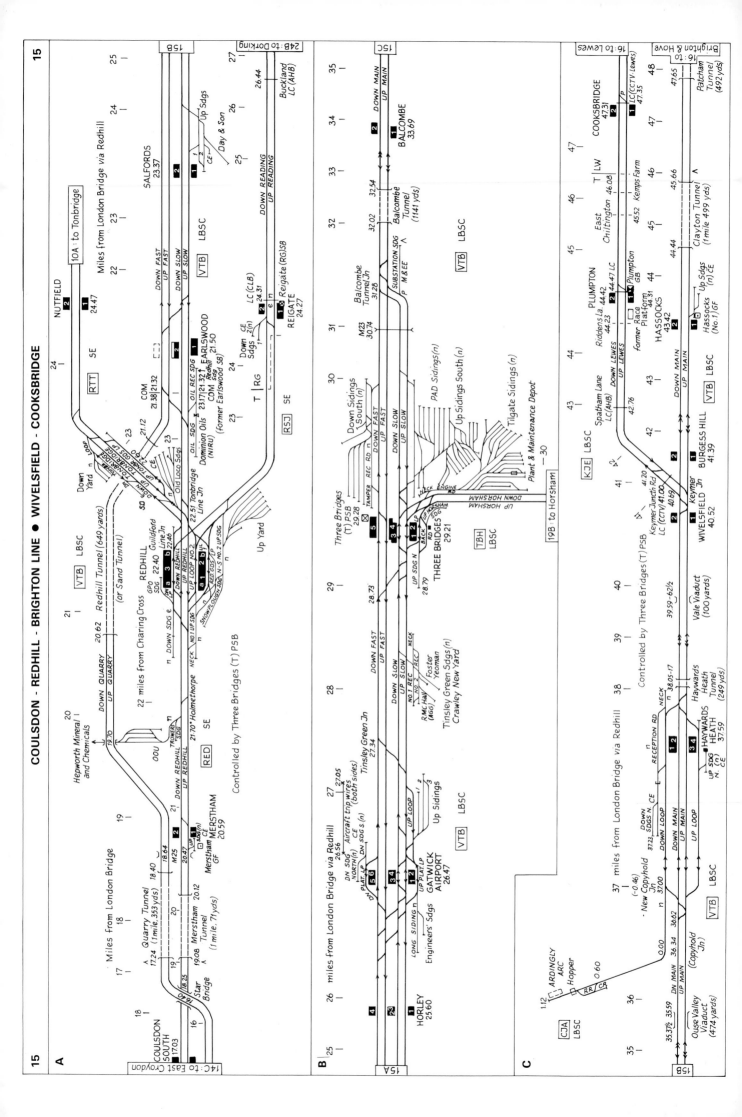

COULSDON - REDHILL - BRIGHTON LINE ● WIVELSFIELD - COOKSBRIDGE

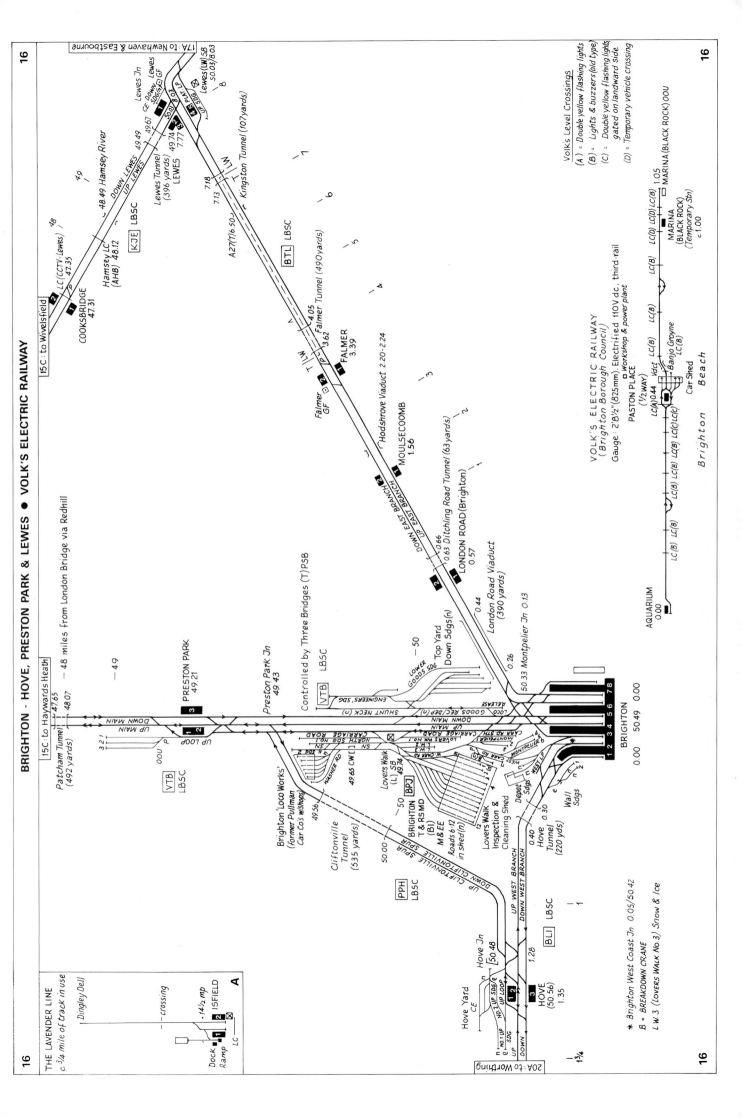

BRIGHTON - HOVE, PRESTON PARK & LEWES ● VOLK'S ELECTRIC RAILWAY

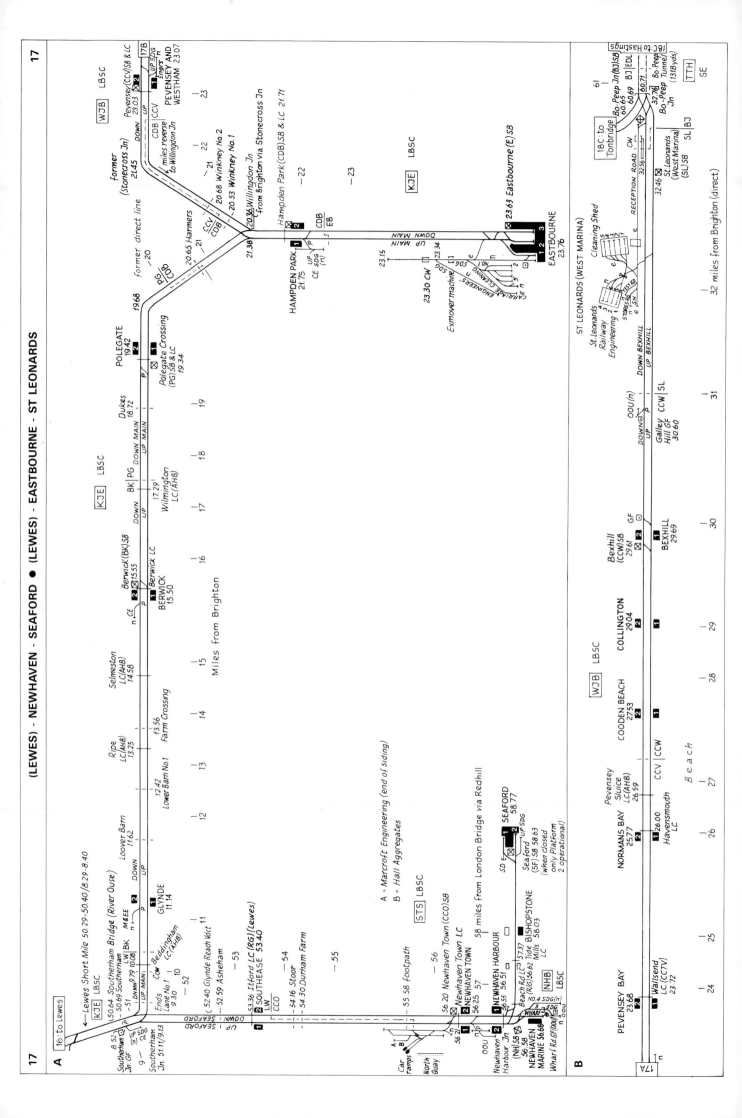

(LEWES) - NEWHAVEN - SEAFORD ● (LEWES) - EASTBOURNE - ST LEONARDS

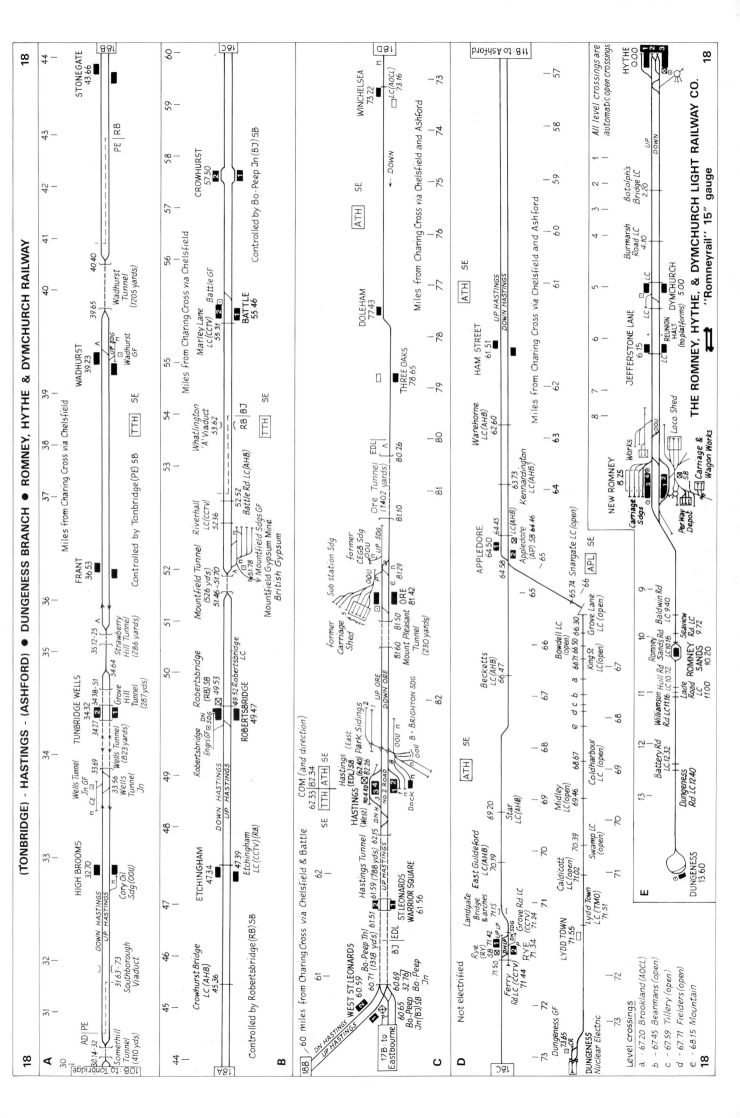

(TONBRIDGE) - HASTINGS - (ASHFORD) ● DUNGENESS BRANCH ● ROMNEY, HYTHE & DYMCHURCH RAILWAY

THE ROMNEY, HYTHE, & DYMCHURCH LIGHT RAILWAY CO.

"Romneyrail" 15" gauge

All level crossings are automatic open crossings

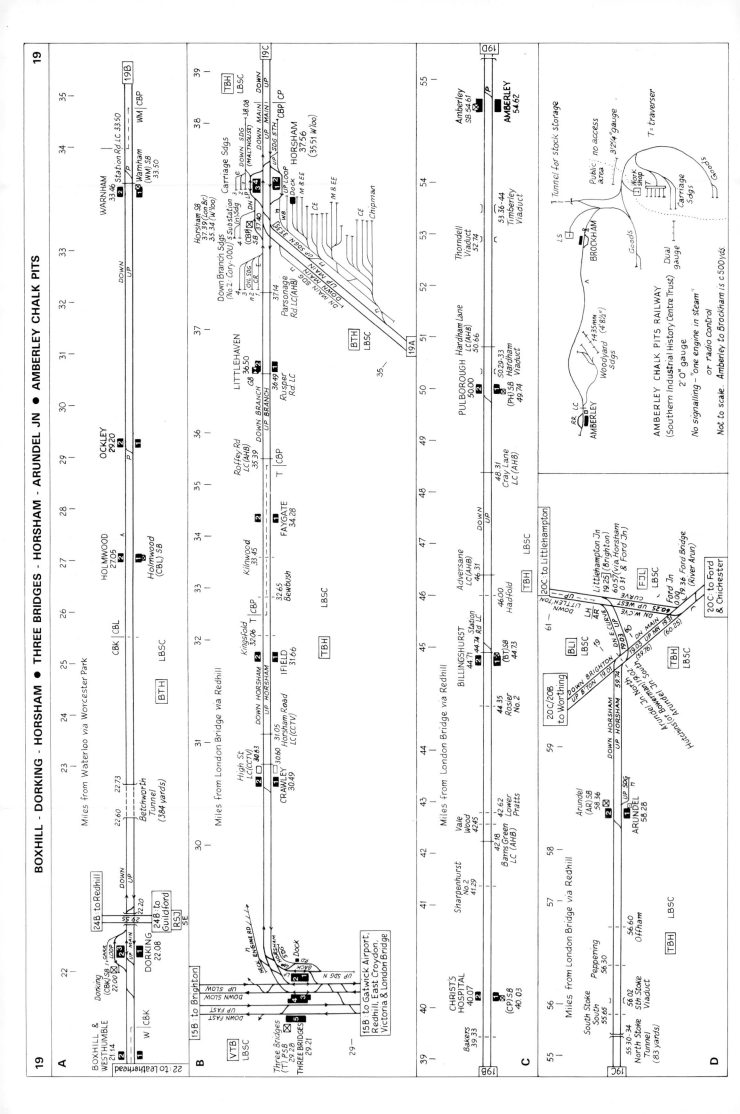

BOXHILL - DORKING - HORSHAM ● THREE BRIDGES - HORSHAM - ARUNDEL JN ● AMBERLEY CHALK PITS

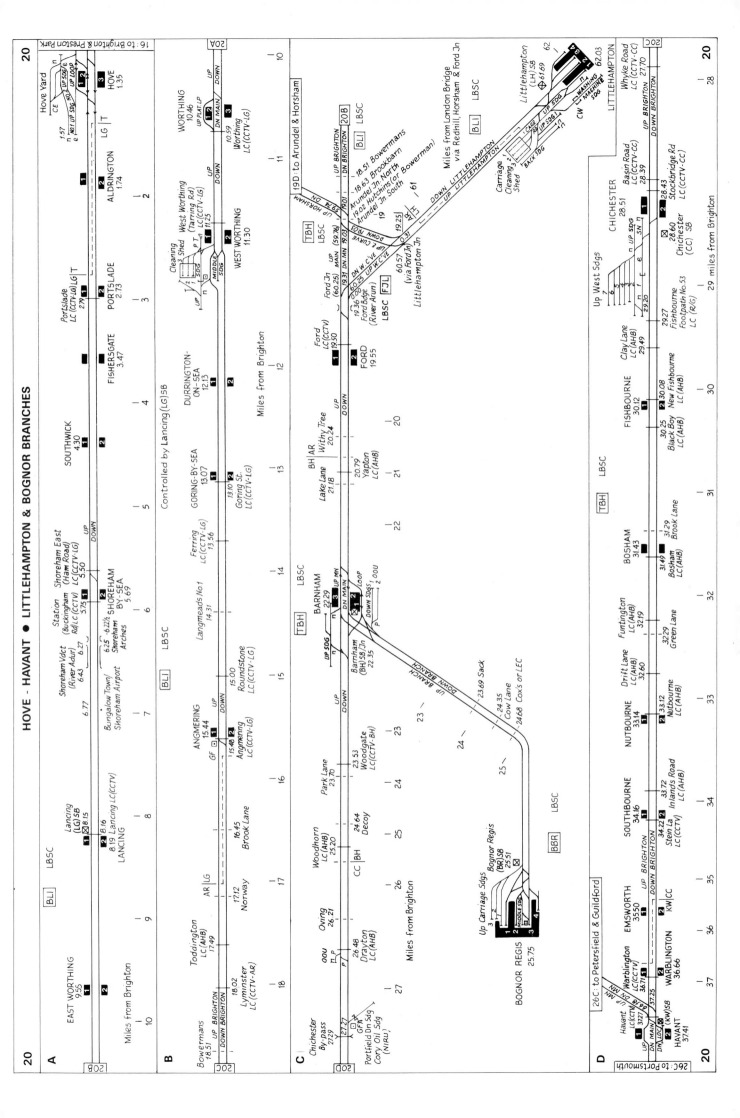

HOVE - HAVANT ● LITTLEHAMPTON & BOGNOR BRANCHES

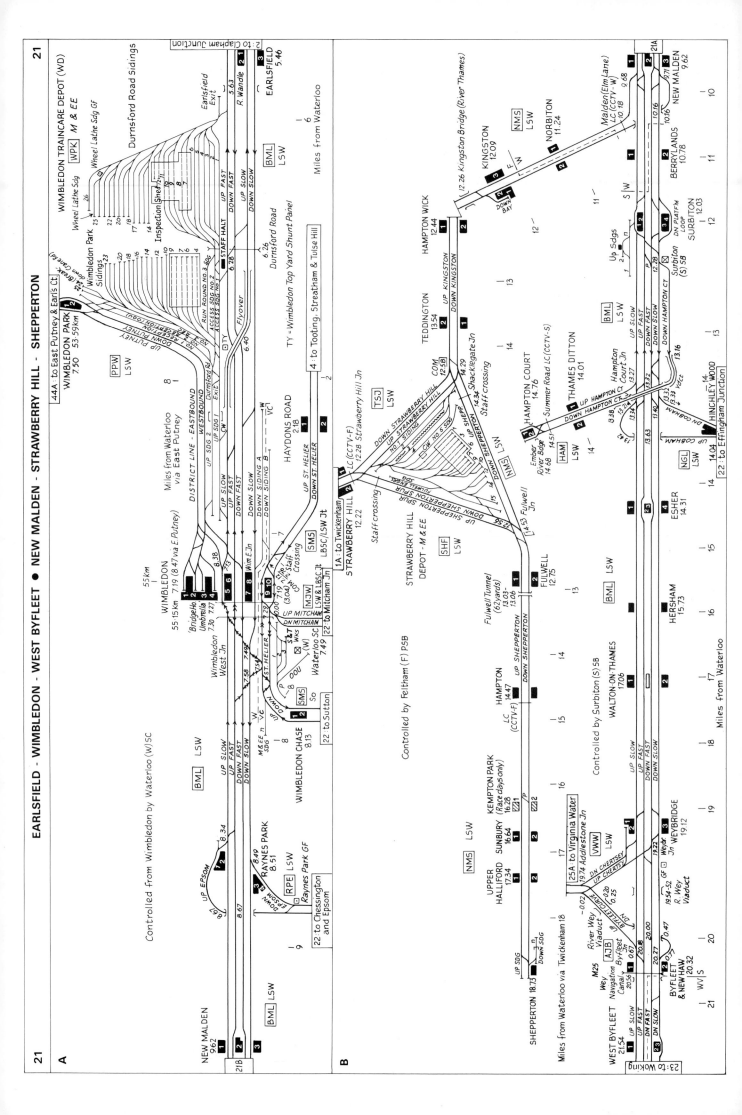

EARLSFIELD - WIMBLEDON - WEST BYFLEET ● NEW MALDEN - STRAWBERRY HILL - SHEPPERTON

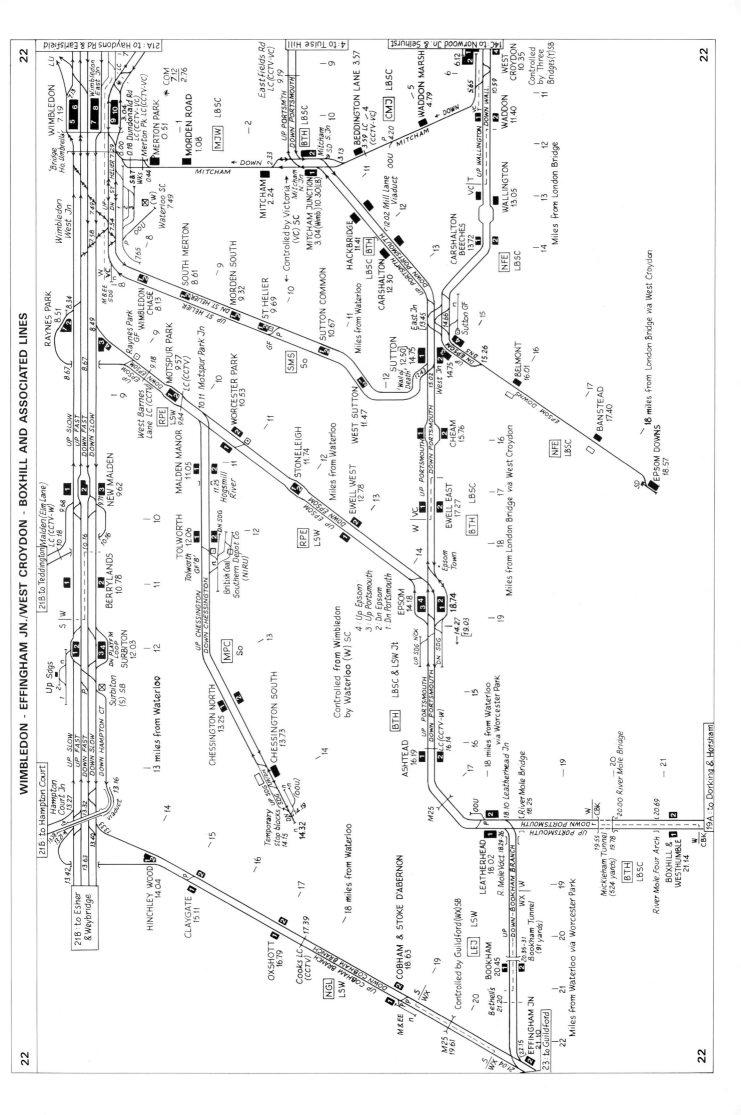

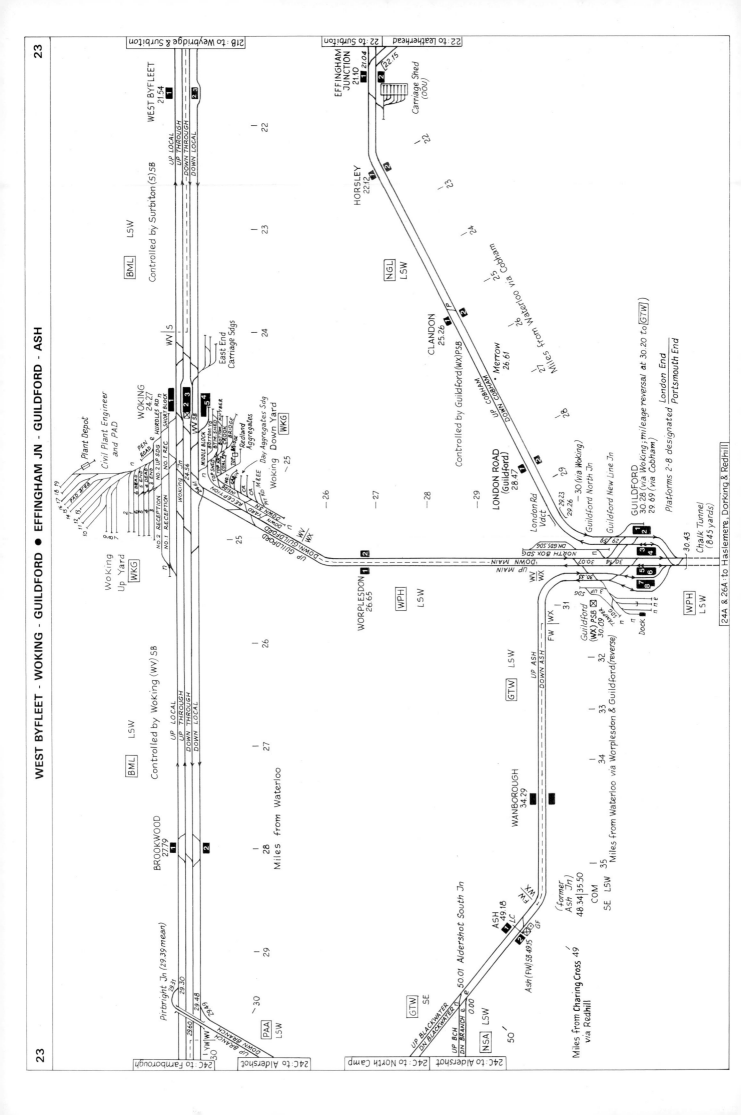

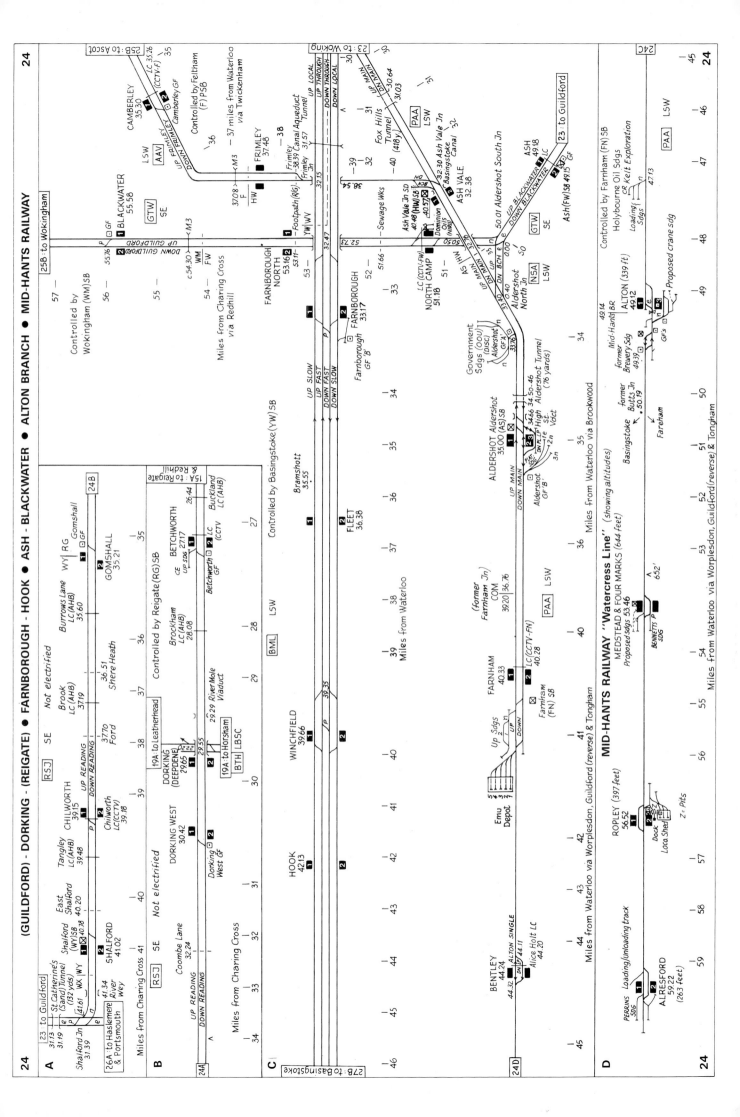

(GUILDFORD) - DORKING - (REIGATE) ● FARNBOROUGH - HOOK ● ASH - BLACKWATER ● ALTON BRANCH ● MID-HANTS RAILWAY

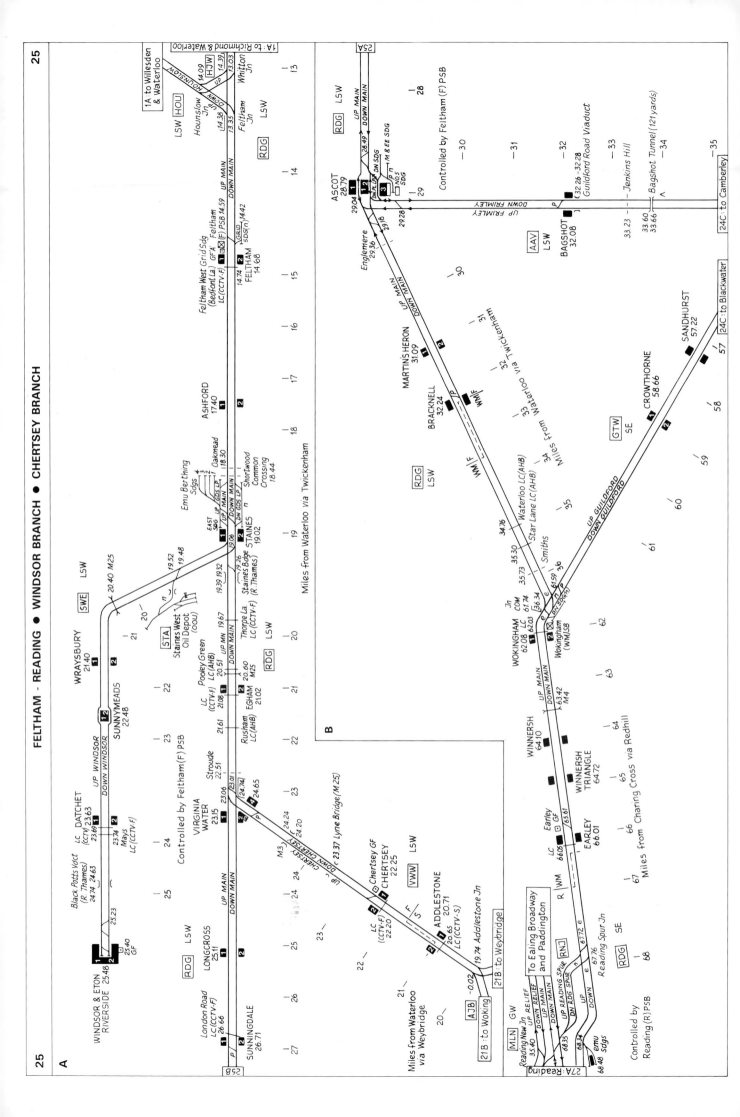

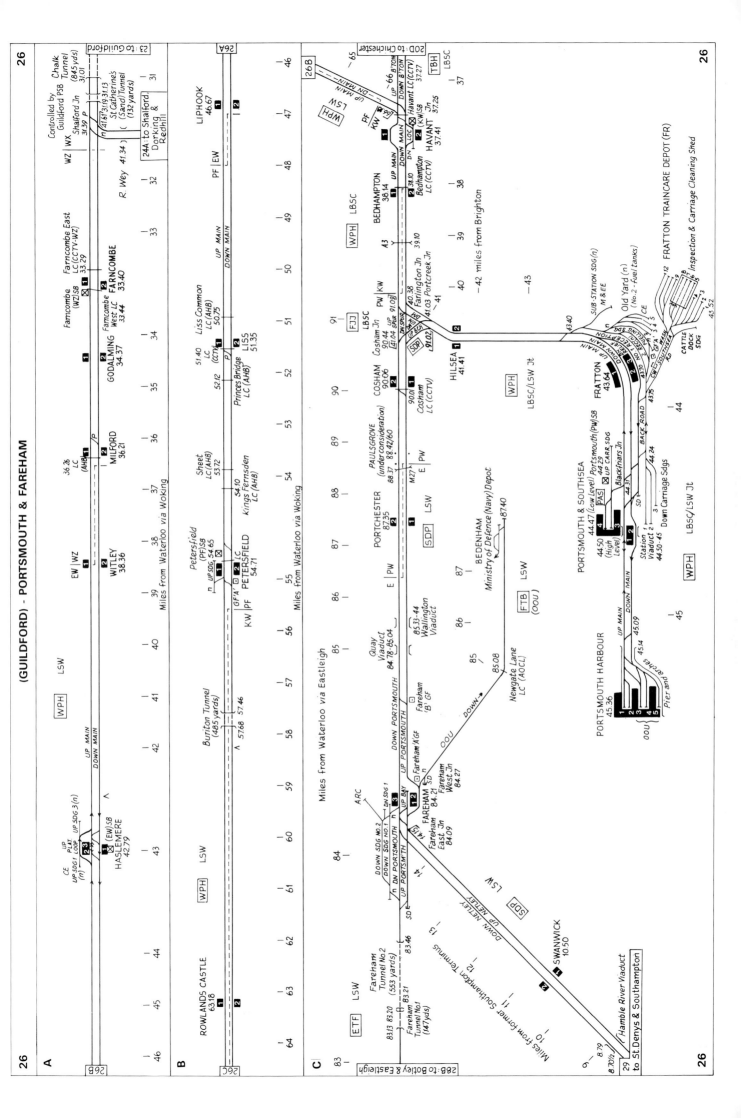

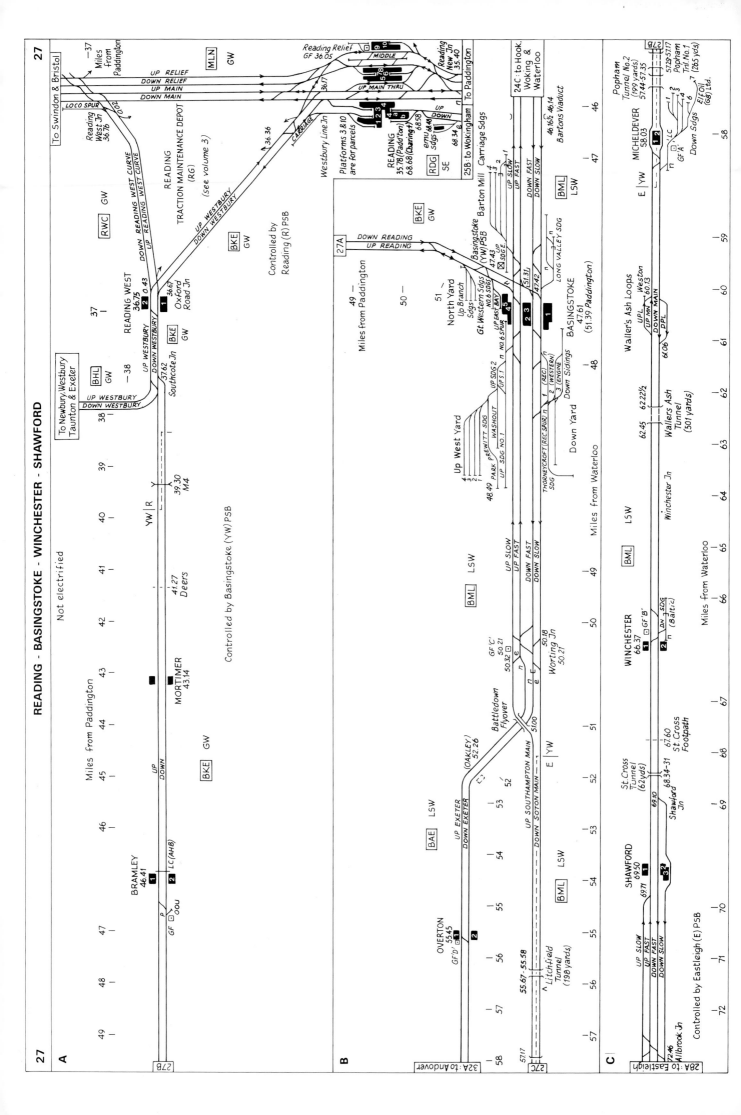

READING - BASINGSTOKE - WINCHESTER - SHAWFORD

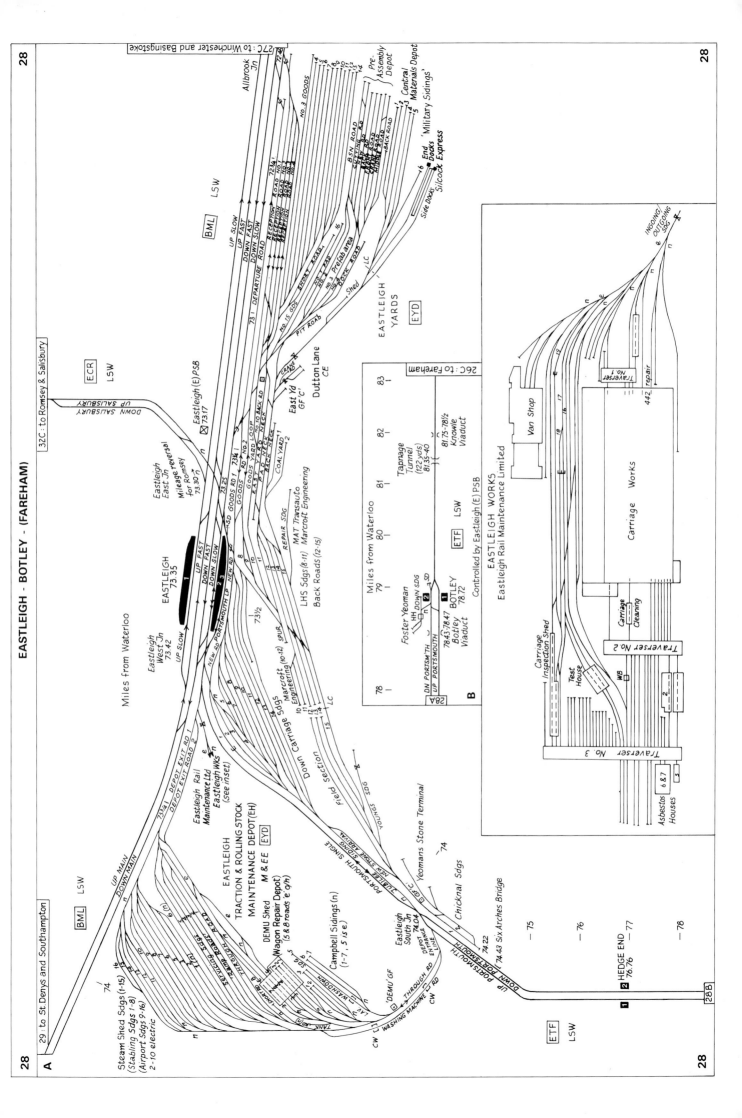

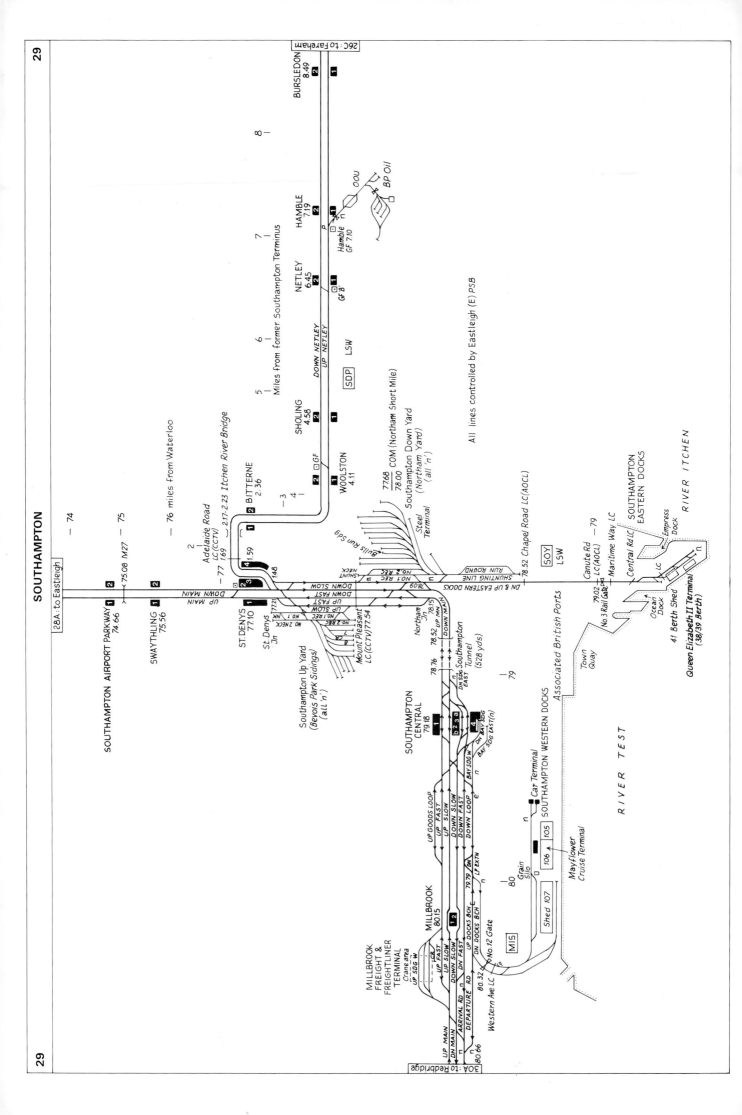

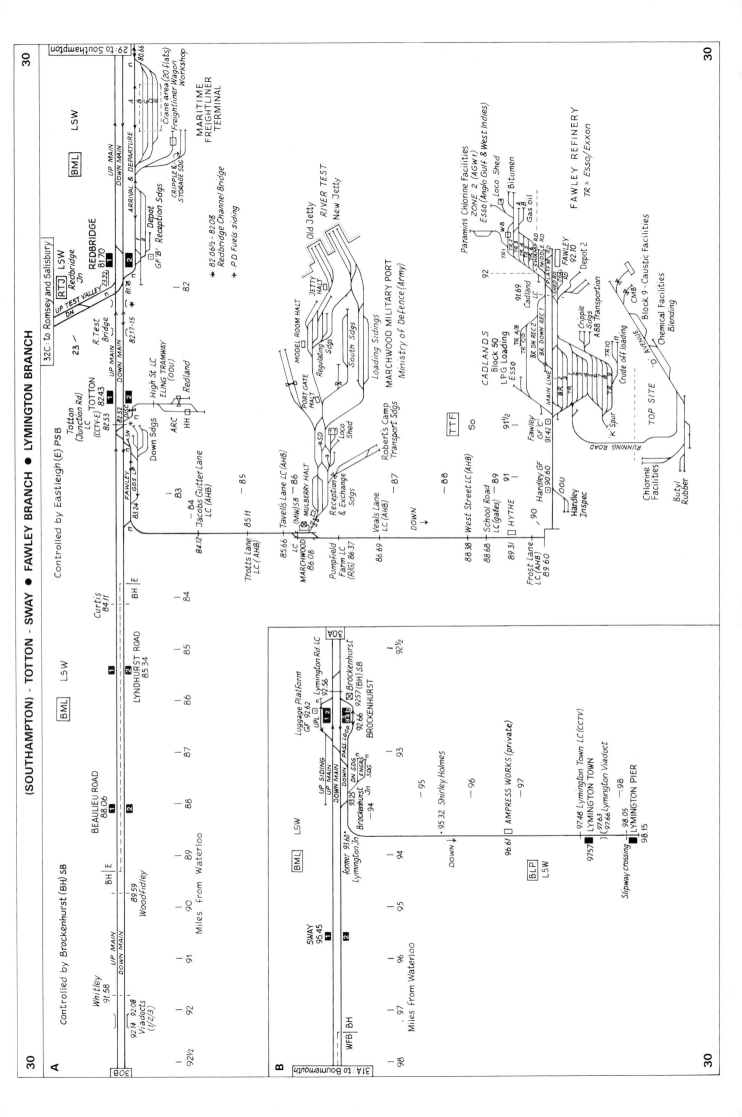

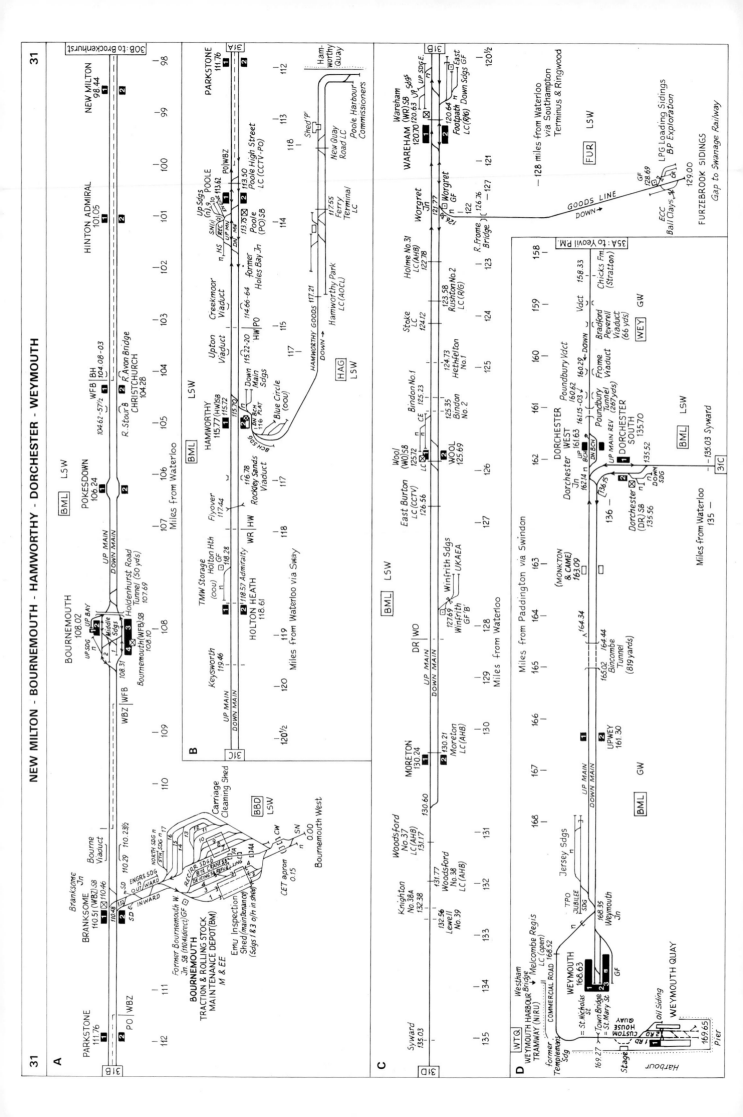

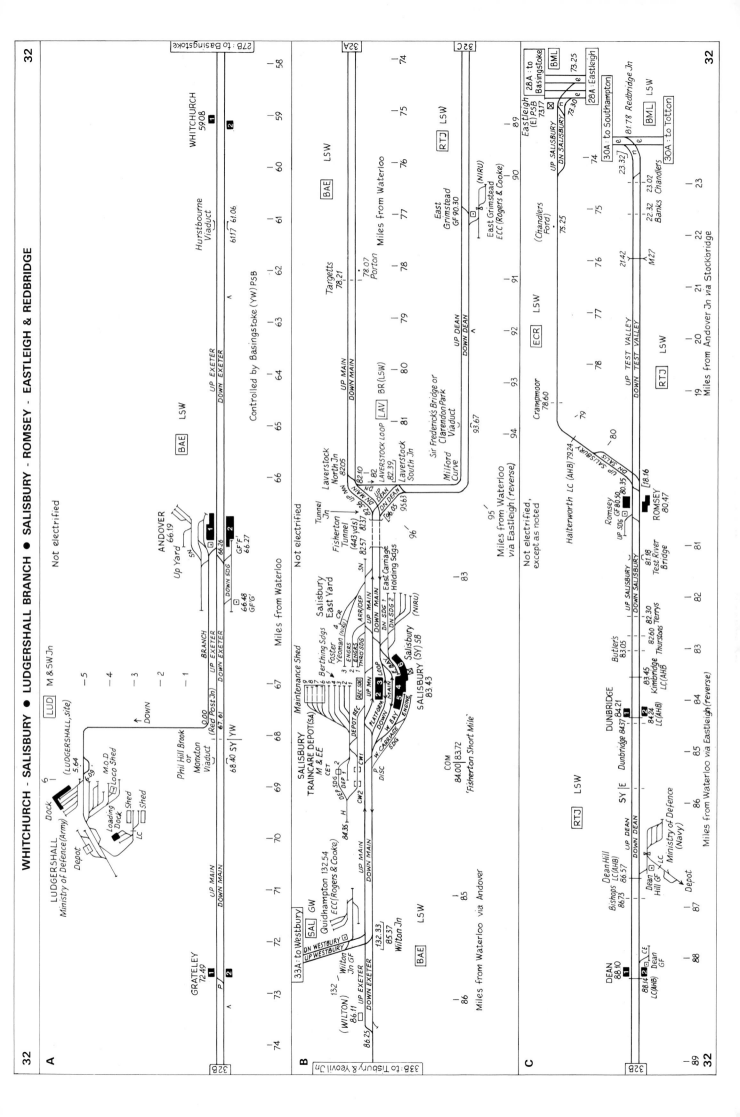

WESTBURY - (WILTON) ● (WILTON) - YEOVIL JN. - CREWKERNE

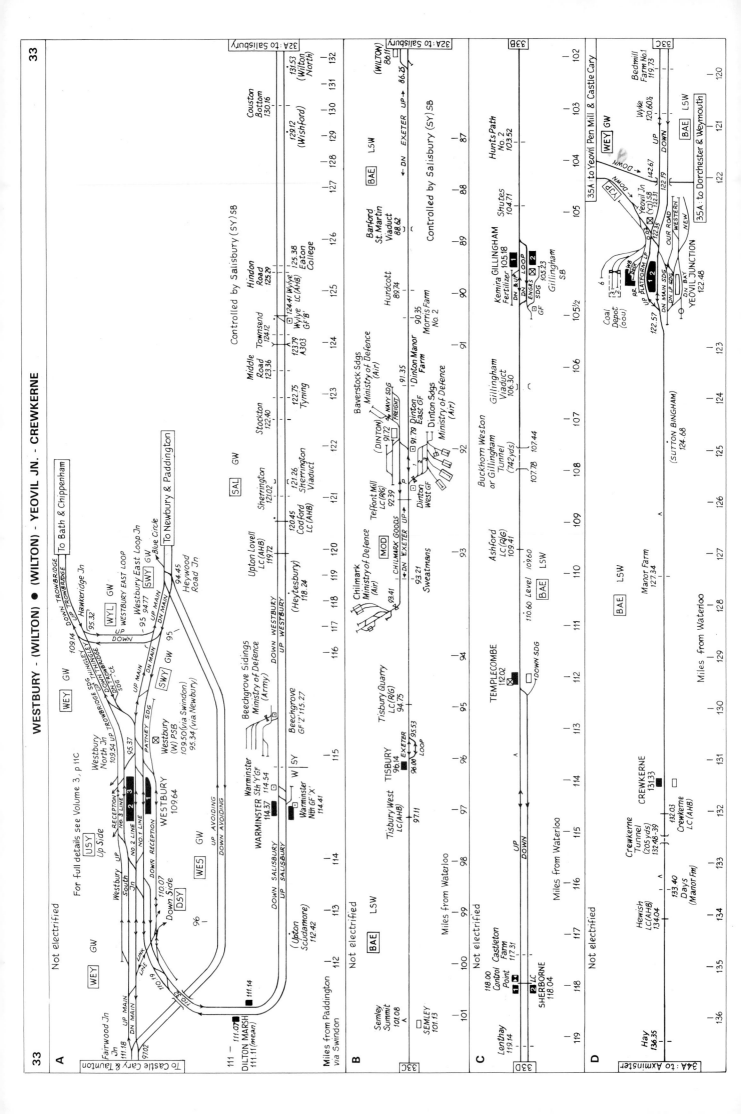

CHARD JUNCTION - EXETER • EXMOUTH BRANCH • SEATON TRAMWAY • BICTON WOODLAND RAILWAY

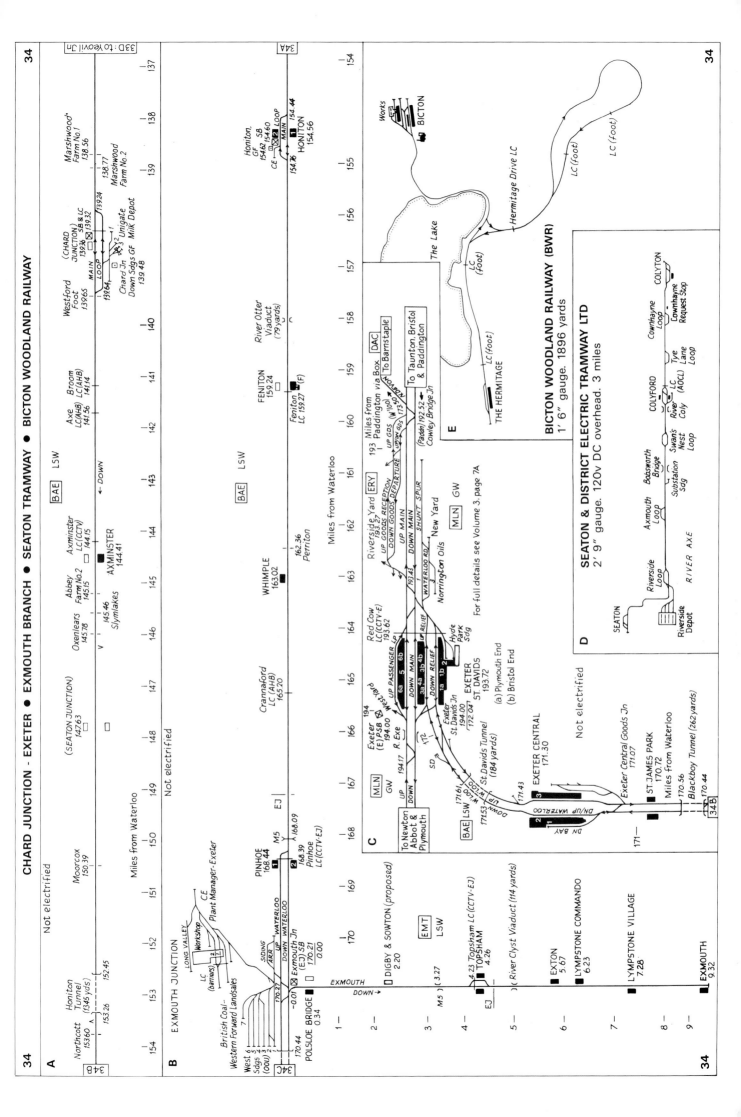

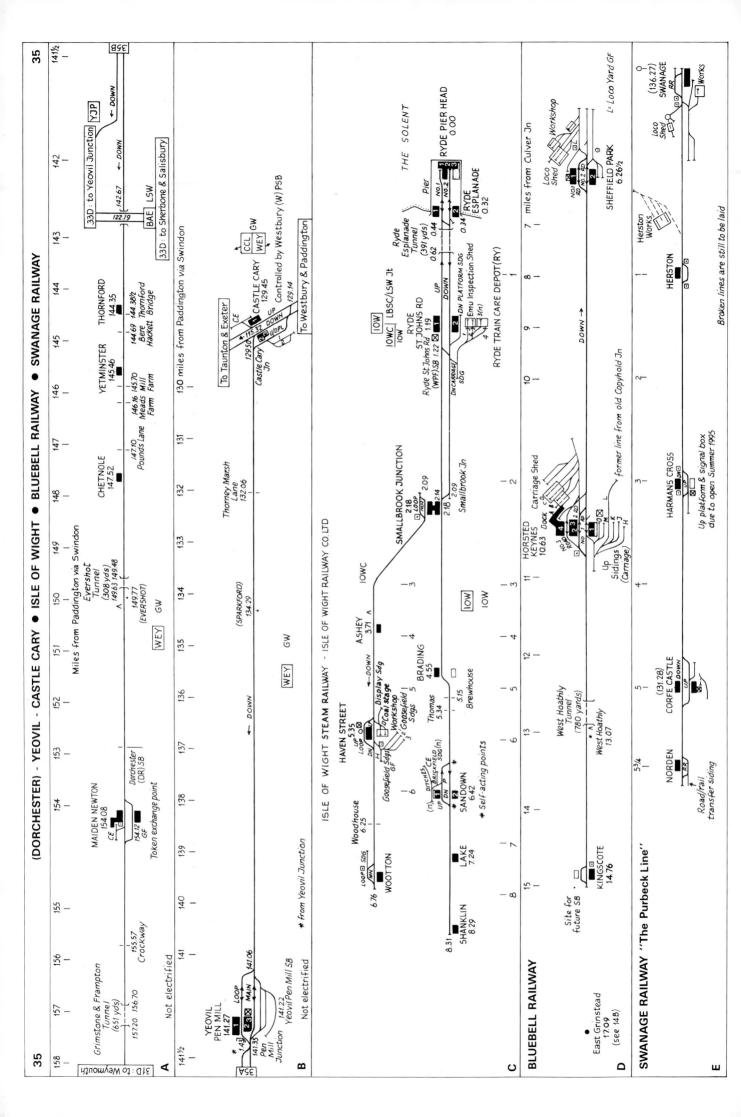

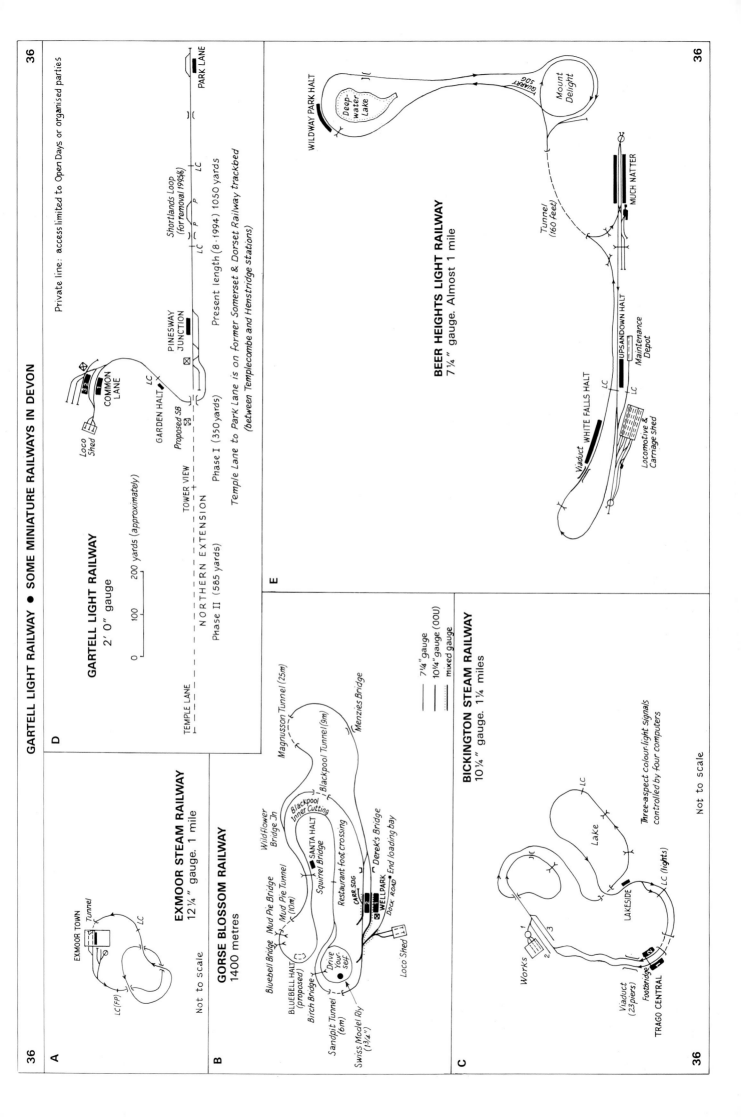

GARTELL LIGHT RAILWAY ● SOME MINIATURE RAILWAYS IN DEVON

A

EXMOOR TOWN

Tunnel

LC

LC (FP)

EXMOOR STEAM RAILWAY
12¼" gauge. 1 mile

Not to scale

B

GORSE BLOSSOM RAILWAY
1400 metres

Magnusson Tunnel (25m)

Menzies Bridge

Blackpool Tunnel (9m)

Blackpool Inner Cutting

WildFlower Bridge Jn

Bluebell Bridge   Mud Pie Bridge

Mud Pie Tunnel (10m)

SANTA HALT

Squirrel Bridge

Restaurant foot crossing

Derek's Bridge

CARR. SDG

WELLPARK

Dock Road   End loading bay

Loco Shed

BLUEBELL HALT (proposed)

Birch Bridge

Sandpit Tunnel (6m)

Swiss Model Rly (1¾")

Drive Your-self

7¼" gauge

10¼" gauge (OOU)

mixed gauge

C

BICKINGTON STEAM RAILWAY
10¼" gauge. 1¼ miles

Works

1 2 3

LC

Lake

LAKESIDE

LC (lights)

Viaduct (23 piers)

Footbridge

TRAGO CENTRAL

Three-aspect colour-light signals controlled by four computers

Not to scale

D

Private line: access limited to Open Days or organised parties

GARTELL LIGHT RAILWAY
2' 0" gauge

Loco Shed

COMMON LANE

LC

GARDEN HALT

Proposed SB

TOWER VIEW

PINESWAY JUNCTION

Shortlands Loop (for removal 1995?)

LC   P   P   LC

PARK LANE

Present length (8-1994) 1050 yards

Temple Lane to Park Lane is on former Somerset & Dorset Railway trackbed (between Templecombe and Henstridge stations)

NORTHERN EXTENSION

TEMPLE LANE

Phase I (350 yards)   Phase II (585 yards)

0   100   200 yards (approximately)

E

BEER HEIGHTS LIGHT RAILWAY
7¼" gauge. Almost 1 mile

WILDWAY PARK HALT

Deep-water Lake

QUARRY SDG

Mount Delight

Tunnel (160 feet)

MUCH NATTER

Viaduct   WHITE FALLS HALT

LC

UPSANDOWN HALT

LC

Maintenance Depot

Locomotive & Carriage shed

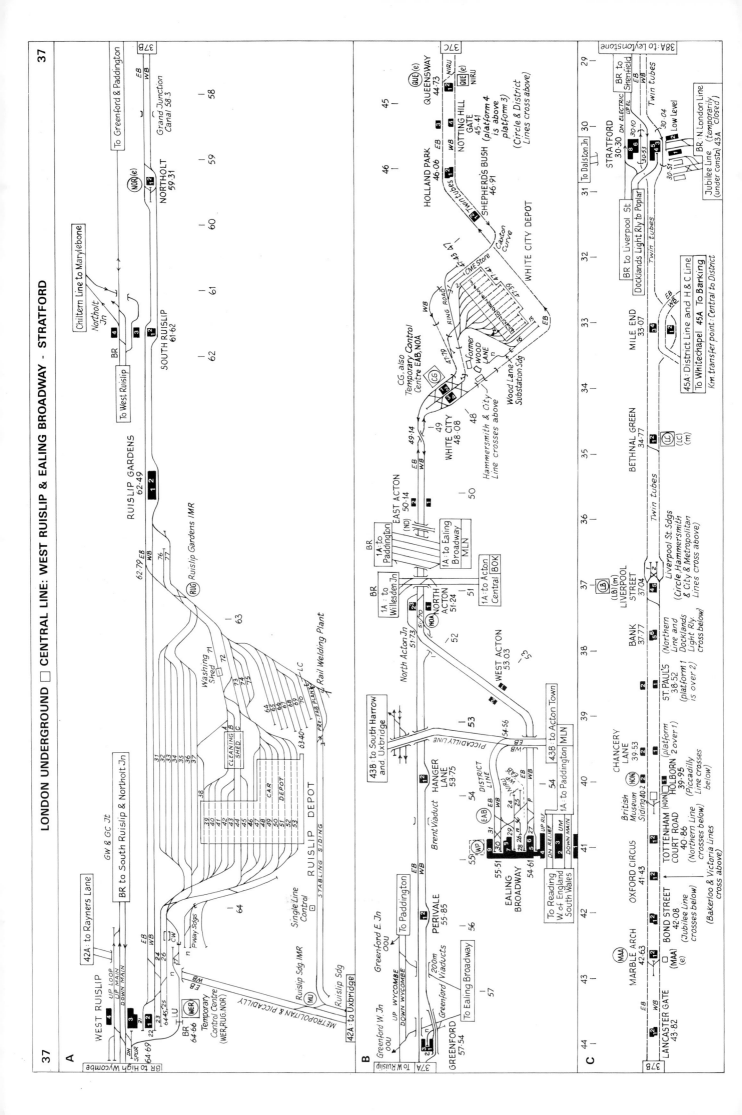

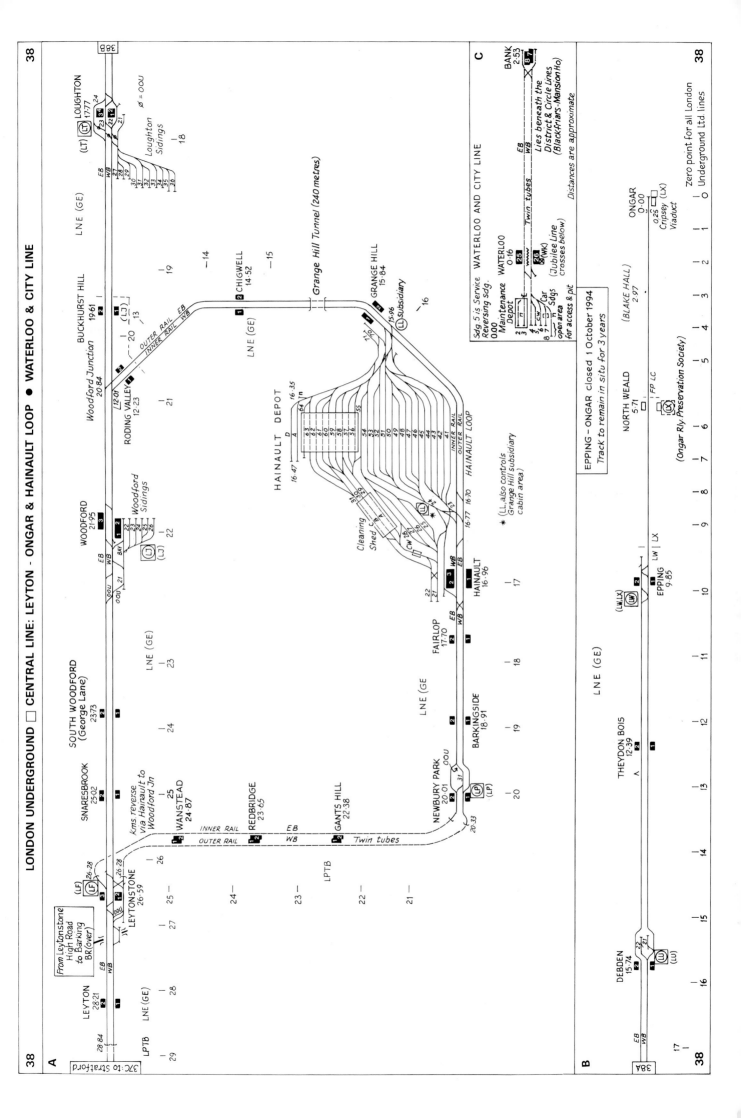

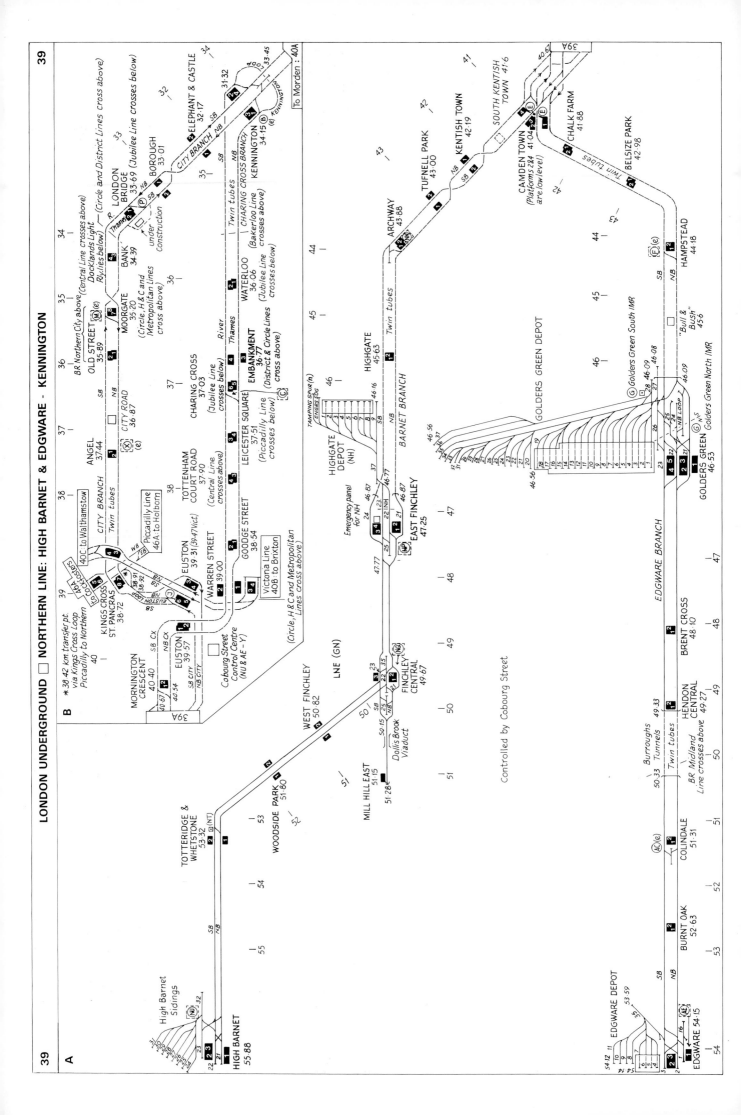

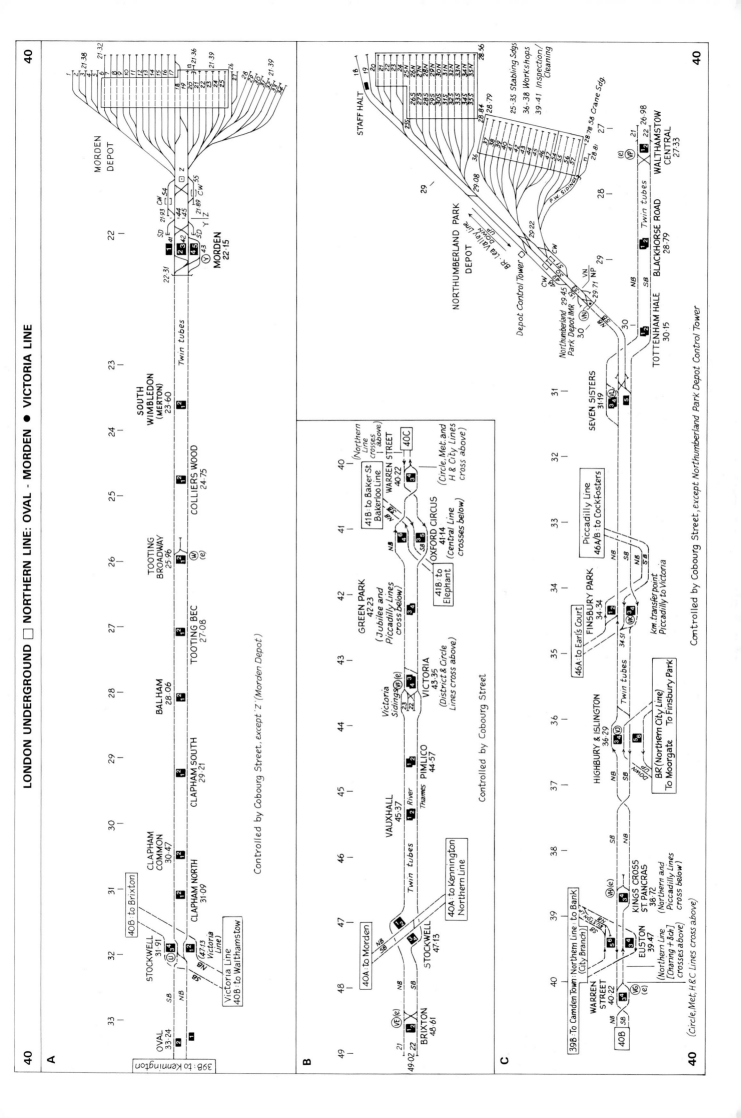

LONDON UNDERGROUND □ NORTHERN LINE: OVAL - MORDEN ● VICTORIA LINE

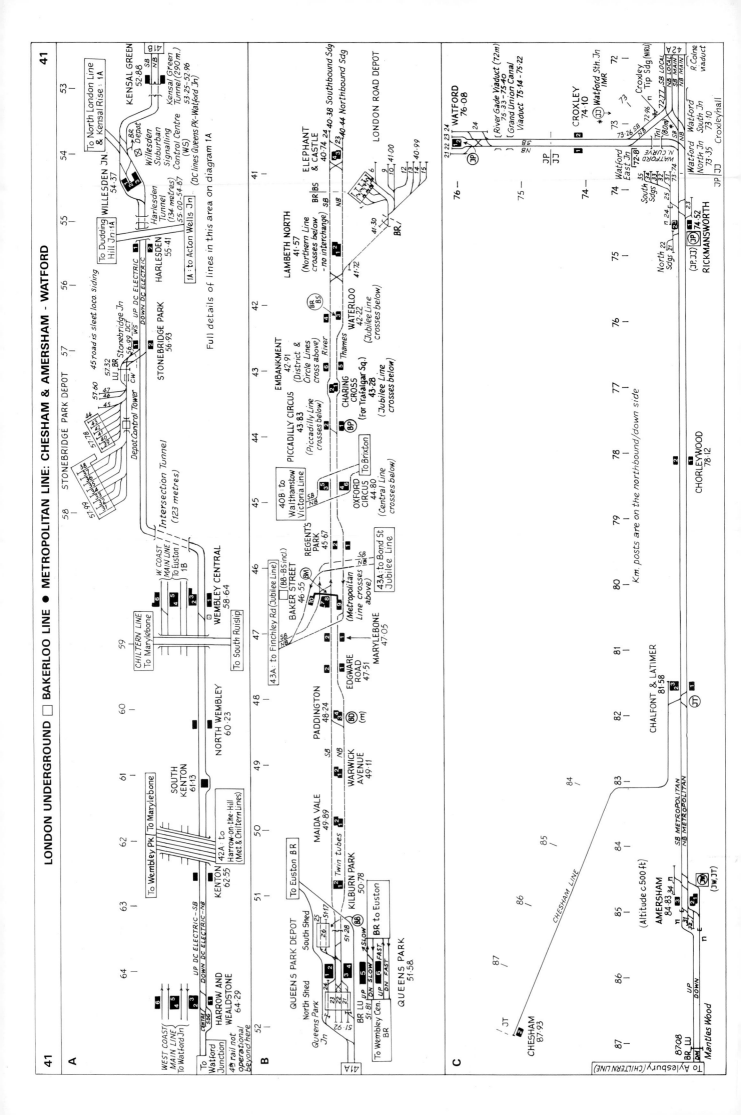

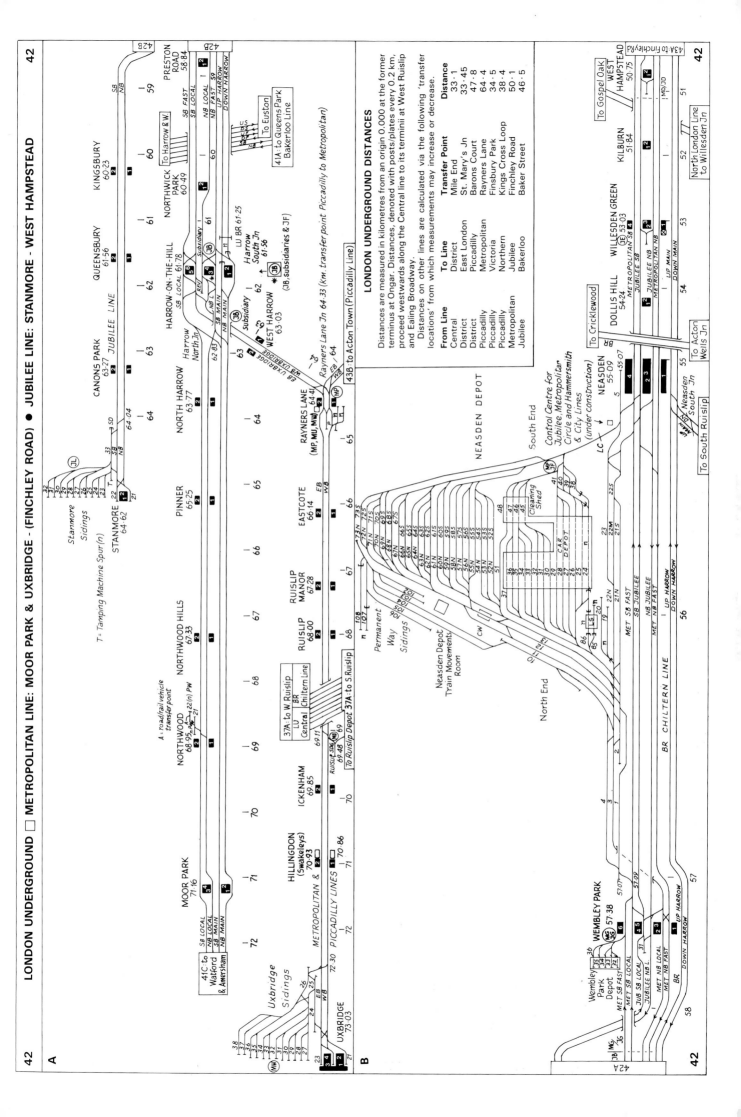

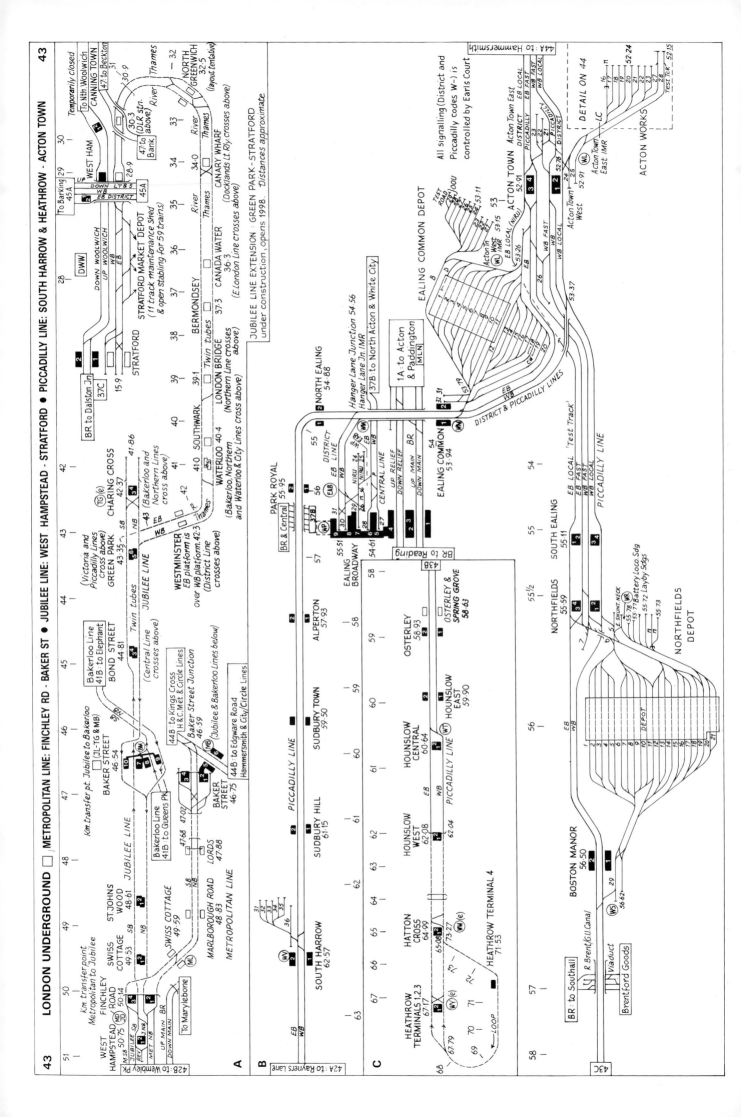

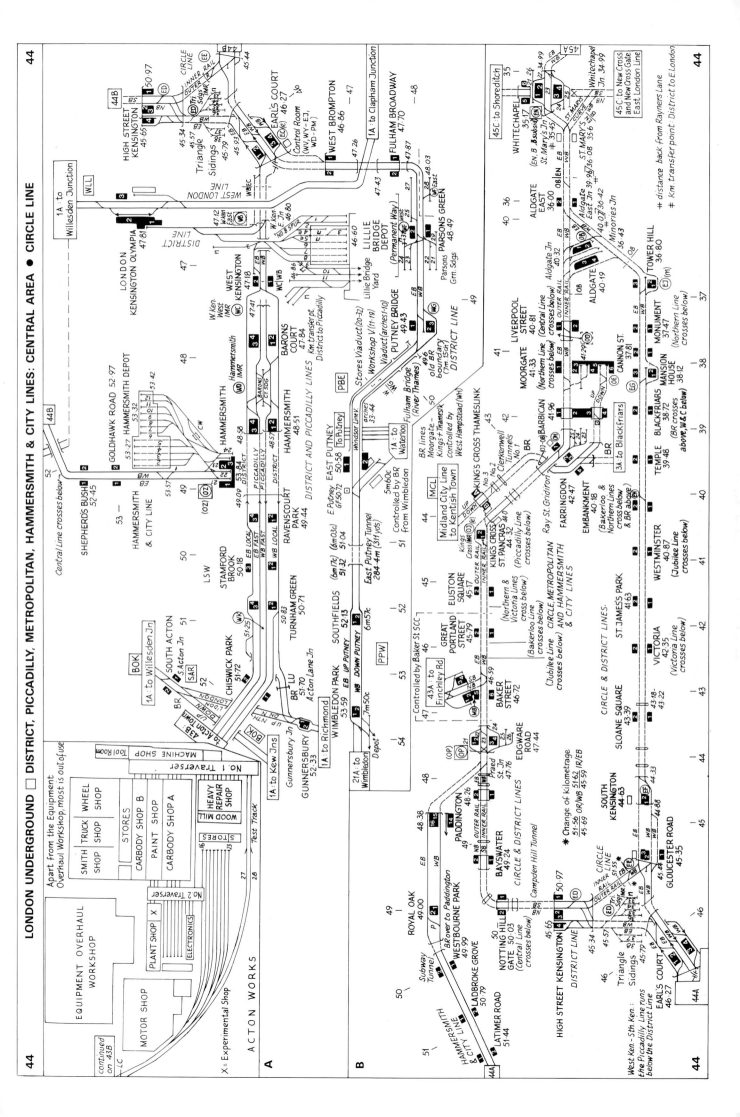

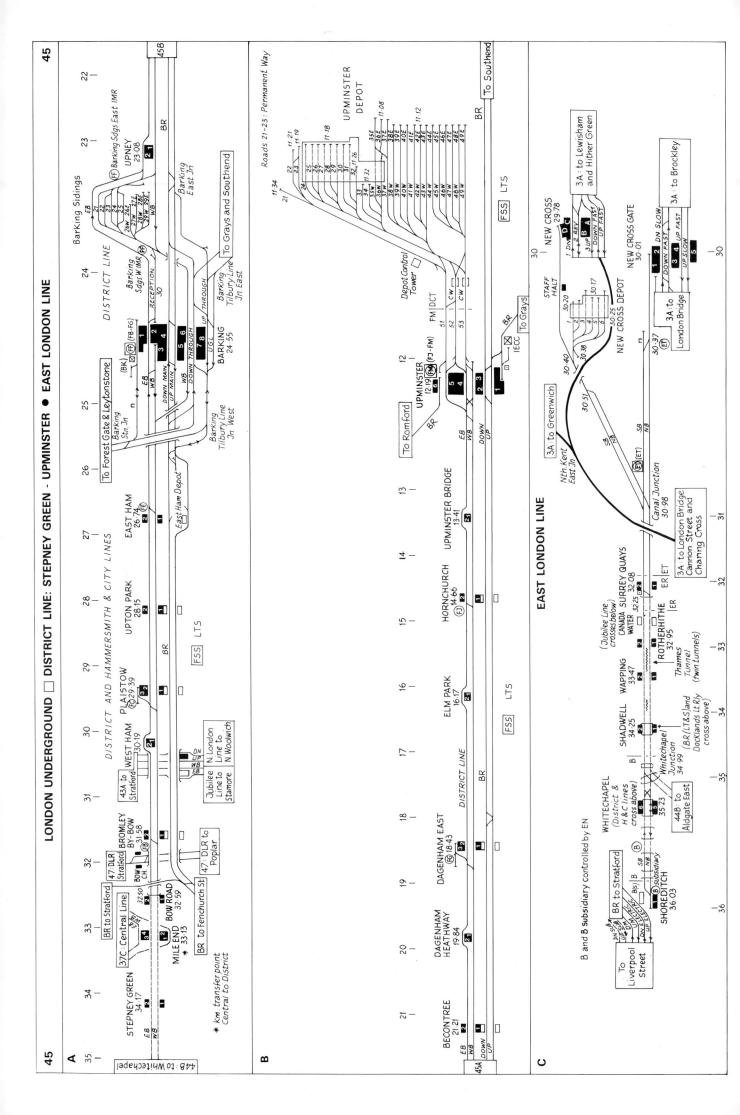

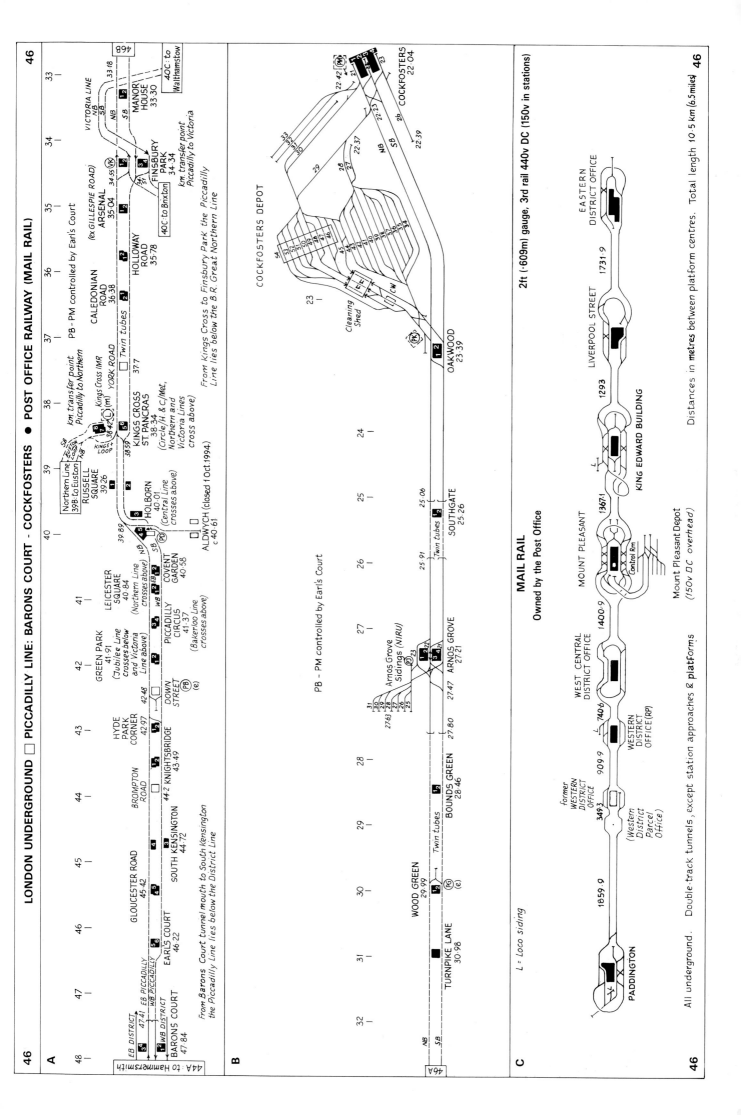

A

VICTORIA LINE
NB SB
NB SB
MANOR HOUSE 33·30
33·18

40C: to Walthamstow

km transfer point Piccadilly to Victoria

FINSBURY PARK 34·34

(ex GILLESPIE ROAD)
ARSENAL 35·04

40C: to Brixton

PB - PM controlled by Earl's Court

CALEDONIAN ROAD 36·38

HOLLOWAY ROAD 35·78

km transfer point Piccadilly to Northern

Kings Cross IMR
YORK ROAD 37·7
Twin tubes

From Kings Cross to Finsbury Park the Piccadilly Line lies below the B.R. Great Northern Line

Northern Line 39B: to Euston
RUSSELL SQUARE 39·26

KINGS CROSS ST. PANCRAS 38·34
KINGS CROSS LOOP
38·59
38·42 (m)
(Circle/H. & C./Met., Northern and Victoria Lines cross above)

HOLBORN 40·01
(Central Line crosses above)

ALDWYCH (closed 1 Oct.1994). c 40·61

LEICESTER SQUARE 40·84
(Northern Line crosses above)

COVENT GARDEN 40·58

GREEN PARK 41·91
(Jubilee Line crosses below and Victoria Line above)

PICCADILLY CIRCUS 41·37
(Bakerloo Line crosses above)

HYDE PARK CORNER 42·97

DOWN STREET 42·48 (e)

BROMPTON ROAD 43·49
KNIGHTSBRIDGE 43·49
44·2

GLOUCESTER ROAD 45·42

SOUTH KENSINGTON 44·72

EARLS COURT 46·22

From Barons Court tunnel mouth to South Kensington the Piccadilly Line lies below the District Line

EB DISTRICT
EB PICCADILLY 47·41
WB PICCADILLY
WB DISTRICT
BARONS COURT 47·84

44A: to Hammersmith

B

COCKFOSTERS DEPOT

22·42 (M)
COCKFOSTERS 22·04
33
32
30
29
28
27
22·37
22·23
NB
SB
22·39

Cleaning Shed
C E
CW
(K)
OAKWOOD 23·39
54 53 52 51 50 49 48 47 46 45 44 43 42 41 40 39 38 37 36 35 34

23

From Kings Cross to Finsbury Park the Piccadilly Line lies below the B.R. Great Northern Line

PB - PM controlled by Earl's Court

SOUTHGATE 25·26
25·06
Twin tubes
25·91

Arnos Grove Sidings (NIRU)
(PD) 23
31 30 29 28 27 26 25
2763
ARNOS GROVE 27·21
27·47
27·80

BOUNDS GREEN 28·46

WOOD GREEN 29·99
(K) (e)

TURNPIKE LANE 30·98

Twin tubes

NB
SB
46A

C

2ft (·609m) gauge, 3rd rail 440v DC (150v in stations)

MAIL RAIL
Owned by the Post Office

EASTERN DISTRICT OFFICE

LIVERPOOL STREET 1731·9

KING EDWARD BUILDING

MOUNT PLEASANT
1293
1400·9
Control Rm

WEST CENTRAL DISTRICT OFFICE

Mount Pleasant Depot
(150v DC overhead)

WESTERN DISTRICT OFFICE (RP)
740·6
909·9

former WESTERN DISTRICT OFFICE
(Western District Parcel Office)
349·3

PADDINGTON 1859·9

L = Loco siding

All underground. Double-track tunnels, except station approaches & platforms.

Distances in metres between platform centres. Total length 10·5 km (6·5 miles)

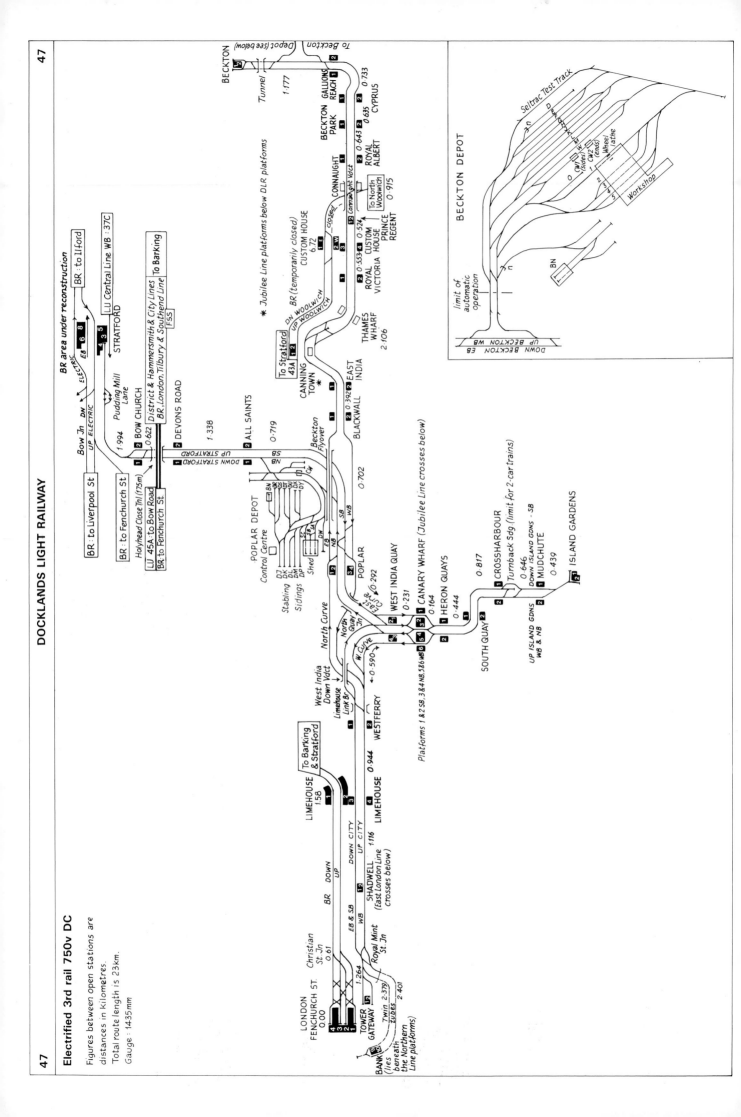

DOCKLANDS LIGHT RAILWAY

INDEX TO STATIONS, *LINES* and selected other places

ABBEY WOOD	5
ACTON CENTRAL	1A
ACTON MAIN LINE	1A
ACTON TOWN	43B
Acton Works	43B, 44
ADDISCOMBE	4
ADDLESTONE	25A
ADISHAM	13
ALBANY PARK	5
ALDERSHOT	24C
ALDGATE	44B
ALDGATE EAST	44B
ALDRINGTON	20A
Aldwych	46A
ALL SAINTS	47
ALPERTON	43B
ALRESFORD	24D
ALTON	24D
AMBERLEY	19C, 19E
AMBERLEY CHALK PITS RLY	19E
AMERSHAM	41C
Ampress Works	30B
ANDOVER	32A
ANERLEY	4
ANGEL	39B
Angerstein Wharf	5
ANGMERING	20A
APPLEDORE	18D
AQUARIUM	16
ARCHWAY	39A
Ardingly	15C
ARNOS GROVE	46B
ARSENAL	46A
ARUNDEL	19D
ASCOT	25B
ASH	23, 24C
ASH VALE	24C
ASHEY	35C
ASHFORD (Kent)	11B
ASHFORD (Surrey)	25A
ASHTEAD	22
ASHURST	14B
AXMINSTER	34A
AYLESFORD	7
AYLESHAM	13
BAGSHOT	25B
BAKER STREET	41B, 43A, 44B
BAKERLOO LINE	41A, 41B
BALCOMBE	15B
BALHAM	4, 40A
BANK	37C, 38C, 39B, 47
BANSTEAD	22
BARBICAN	44B
BARKING	45A
BARKINGSIDE	38A
BARMING	7
BARNEHURST	5
BARNES	1A
BARNES BRIDGE	1A
BARNHAM	20C
BARONS COURT	44A, 46A
BASINGSTOKE	27B
BAT & BALL	6A
BATTERSEA PARK	2
BATTLE	18B
Baverstock	33B
BAYSWATER	44B
BEARSTED	7, 11A
BEAULIEU ROAD	30A
BECKENHAM HILL	4
BECKENHAM JUNCTION	4
BECKTON	47
BECKTON PARK	47
BECONTREE	45B
BEDDINGTON LANE	22
Bedenham	26C
BEDHAMPTON	26C
Beechgrove Sidings	33A
BEER HEIGHTS LIGHT RLY	36E
BEKESBOURNE	9B
BELLINGHAM	4
BELMONT	22
BELSIZE PARK	39A
BELTRING	10C
BELVEDERE	5
BENTLEY	24C
BERMONDSEY	43A
BERRYLANDS	21B, 22
BERWICK	17A
BETCHWORTH	24B
BETHNAL GREEN	37C
Betteshanger	9A
BEXHILL	17B
BEXLEY	5
BEXLEYHEATH	5
BICKINGTON STEAM RAILWAY	36C
BICKLEY	6A
BICTON	34E
BICTON WOODLAND RLY	34E
BILLINGSHURST	19C
BIRCHINGTON ON SEA	9A
BIRKBECK	4
BISHOPSTONE	17A
BITTERNE	29
BLACKFRIARS	3A, 44B
BLACKHEATH	5
BLACKHORSE ROAD	40C
BLACKWALL	47
BLACKWATER	24C
Blake Hall	38B
BLUEBELL RAILWAY	35D
BOGNOR REGIS	20C
BOND STREET	37C, 43A
BOOKHAM	22
Bo-Peep Jn	17B
BOROUGH	39B
BOROUGH GREEN & WROTHAM	7
BOSHAM	20D
BOSTON MANOR	43B
BOTLEY	28B
BOUNDS GREEN	46B
BOURNEMOUTH	31A
BOW CHURCH	47
BOW ROAD	45A
BOXHILL & WESTHUMBLE	19A, 22
BRACKNELL	25B
BRADING	35C
BRAMLEY	27A
BRANKSOME	31A
BRENT CROSS	39A
BRENTFORD	1A
BRIGHTON	16
BRIXTON	3A, 4, 40B
BROADSTAIRS	9A
BROCKENHURST	30B
BROCKHAM	19E
BROCKLEY	3A, 4
BROMLEY-BY-BOW	45A
BROMLEY NORTH	3B
BROMLEY SOUTH	6A
Brompton Road	46A
BROOKWOOD	23
Buckland Junction	13
Bull & Bush	39A
BURGESS HILL	15C
BURNT OAK	39A
BURLESDON	29
BUXTED	14A
BYFLEET & NEW HAW	21B
Cadlands	30A
CALAIS TERMINAL	9D
CALEDONIAN ROAD	46A
CAMDEN TOWN	39A
CANADA WATER	43A, 45C
Canal Junction	45C
CANARY WHARF	43A, 47
CANNING TOWN	43A, 47
CANNON STREET	3A, 44B
CANONS PARK	42A
CANTERBURY EAST	9B
CANTERBURY WEST	9B
CARSHALTON	22
CARSHALTON BEECHES	22
CASTLE CARY	35B
CATERHAM	14C
CATFORD	4
CATFORD BRIDGE	4
CENTRAL LINE	37, 38
CHALFONT & LATIMER	41C
CHALK FARM	39A
CHANCERY LANE	37C
Chard Junction	34A
CHARING	11A
CHARING CROSS	3A, 39B, 41B, 43A
CHARLTON	4
Chart Leacon	11B
CHARTHAM	9B
CHATHAM	8A
CHEAM	22
CHELSFIELD	6A
CHERITON	12A
CHERTSEY	25A
CHESHAM	41C
CHESSINGTON NORTH	22
CHESSINGTON SOUTH	22
CHESTFIELD & SWALECLIFFE	9A
CHETNOLE	35A
CHICHESTER	20D
CHIGWELL	38A
CHILHAM	11B
Chilmark	33B
CHILWORTH	24A
CHIPSTEAD	14C
CHISLEHURST	3B, 6A
CHISLET COLLIERY	9A
CHISWICK	1A
CHISWICK PARK	44A
CHORLEYWOOD	41C
CHRISTCHURCH	31A
CHRIST'S HOSPITAL	19C
CIRCLE LINE	44B
City Road	39B
CITY THAMESLINK	3A
CLANDON	23
CLAPHAM COMMON	40A
CLAPHAM HIGH STREET	2
CLAPHAM JUNCTION	1A, 2, 4
CLAPHAM NORTH	40A
CLAPHAM SOUTH	40A
Clapham Yard	1A, 2
CLAYGATE	22
Cliffe	7
CLOCK HOUSE	4
COBHAM & STOKE D'ABERNON	22
COCKFOSTERS	46B
COLINDALE	39A
COLLIERS WOOD	40A
COLLINGTON	17B
COLYFORD	34D
COLYTON	34D
COMMON LANE	36D
COOKSBRIDGE	15C, 16
COODEN BEACH	17B
COQUELLES	12D
CORFE CASTLE	35E
COSHAM	26C
COULSDON SOUTH	14C, 15A
COVENT GARDEN	46A
COWDEN	14B
CRAWLEY	19B
CRAYFORD	5
CREWKERNE	33D
CROFTON PARK	4
CROSSHARBOUR	47
CROWBOROUGH	14A
CROWHURST	18B
CROWTHORNE	25B
CROXLEY	41C
CRYSTAL PALACE	4
CUXTON	7
CYPRUS	47
DAGENHAM EAST	45B
DAGENHAM HEATHWAY	45B
DARTFORD	5, 7
DATCHET	25A
DEAL	9A
DEAN	32C
DEBDEN	38B
DENMARK HILL	3A, 4
DEPTFORD	3A
DEVONS ROAD	47
DIGBY & SOWTON	34B
DILTON MARSH	33A
Dinton	33B
DISTRICT LINE	43B, 44, 45A, 45B
DOLEHAM	18C
Dollands Moor	11B
DOLLIS HILL	42B
DORCHESTER SOUTH	31D
DORCHESTER WEST	31D
DORKING	19A
DORKING (DEEPDENE)	24B
DORKING WEST	24B
DORMANS	14B
DOVER PRIORY	13
Dover Town Yard	13
Dover Western Docks	13
Down Street	46A
DUMPTON PARK	9A
DUNBRIDGE	32C
DUNGENESS	18D, 18E
DUNTON GREEN	6A
DURRINGTON-ON-SEA	20B
DYMCHURCH	18E
EALING BROADWAY	1A, 37B, 43B
EALING COMMON	43B
EARLEY	25B
EARL'S COURT	44A, 44B, 46A
EARLSFIELD	2, 21A
EARLSWOOD	15A
EAST ACTON	37B
EAST CROYDON	14C
EAST DULWICH	4
EAST FARLEIGH	10C
EAST FINCHLEY	39A
East Grimstead	32B
EAST GRINSTEAD	14B, 35D
EAST HAM	45A
EAST INDIA	47
EAST KENT LIGHT RLY	13
EAST LONDON LINE	45C
EAST MALLING	7
EAST PUTNEY	1A, 44A
EAST WORTHING	20A
EASTBOURNE	17A
EASTCOTE	42A
EASTERN DISTRICT OFFICE	46C
EASTLEIGH	28A
EDEN PARK	4
EDENBRIDGE	10A
EDENBRIDGE TOWN	14B
EDGWARE	39A
EDWARE ROAD	41B, 44B
EFFINGHAM JUNCTION	22, 23
EGHAM	25A
ELEPHANT & CASTLE	3A, 39B, 41B
ELM PARK	45B
ELMERS END	4
ELMSTEAD WOODS	3B
ELTHAM	5
EMBANKMENT	39B, 41B, 44B
EMSWORTH	20D
EPPING	38B
EPSOM	22
EPSOM DOWNS	22
ERIDGE	14B
ERITH	5
ESHER	21B
ETCHINGHAM	18B
Euro Terminal Willesden	1A
EUSTON	39B, 40C
EUSTON SQUARE	44B
EWELL EAST	22
EWELL WEST	22
EXETER CENTRAL	34C
EXETER ST. DAVIDS	34C
EXMOOR STEAM RAILWAY	36A
EXMOUTH	34B
Exmouth Junction	34B
EXTON	34B
EYNSFORD	6A, 7
Eythorne	13
FAIRLOP	38A
Fairwood Jn	33A
FALCONWOOD	5
FALMER	16
FAREHAM	26C
Farlington Jn	26C
FARNBOROUGH	24C
FARNBOROUGH NORTH	24C
FARNCOMBE	26A
FARNHAM	24C
FARNINGHAM ROAD	7
FARRINGDON	3A, 44B
FAVERSHAM	8B
Fawley	30A
FAYGATE	19B
FELTHAM	25A
FENITON	34B
FINCHLEY CENTRAL	39A
FINCHLEY ROAD	43A
FINSBURY PARK	40C, 46A
FISHBOURNE	20D
FISHERSGATE	20A
FLEET	24C
FOLKESTONE CENTRAL	13
FOLKESTONE EAST	13

FOLKESTONE HARBOUR	13
FOLKESTONE TERMINAL	12A
FOLKESTONE WEST	13
FORD	20C
FOREST HILL	4
FRANT	18A
FRATTON	26C
FRÉTHUN-LES-CALAIS	12D
FULHAM BROADWAY	44A
FULWELL	21B
Furzebrook	31C
GALLIONS REACH	47
GANTS HILL	38A
GARDEN HALT	36D
GARTELL LIGHT RAILWAY	36D
GATWICK AIRPORT	15B
GILLINGHAM (Dorset)	33C
GILLINGHAM (Kent)	8A
GIPSY HILL	4
GLOUCESTER ROAD	44B, 46A
GLYNDE	17A
GODALMING	26A
GODSTONE	10A
GOLDERS GREEN	39A
GOLDHAWK ROAD	44A
GOMSHALL	24A
GOODGE STREET	39B
GORING-BY-SEA	20A
GORSE BLOSSOM RAILWAY	36B
Grain	7
GRANGE HILL	38A
GRATELEY	32A
GRAVESEND	7
GREAT PORTLAND STREET	44B
GREEN PARK	40B, 43A, 46A
GREENFORD	37B
GREENHITHE	7
GREENWICH	3A
GROOMBRIDGE	14B
GROVE PARK	3B
GUILDFORD	23
GUNNERSBURY	1A
HACKBRIDGE	22
HAINAULT	38A
HALLING	7
HAM STREET	18D
HAMBLE	29
HAMMERSMITH	44A
HAMMERSMITH & CITY LINE	44, 45A
HAMPDEN PARK	17A
HAMPSTEAD	39A
HAMPTON	21B
HAMPTON COURT	21B
HAMPTON WICK	21B
HAMWORTHY	31B
HANGER LANE	37B
HARLESDEN	1A, 41A
HARMANS CROSS	35E
HARRIETSHAM	11A
HARROW & WEALDSTONE	41A
HARROW-ON-THE-HILL	42A
HASLEMERE	26A
HASSOCKS	15C
HASTINGS	18C
HATTON CROSS	43C
HAVANT	20D, 26C
HAVEN STREET	35C
Hawkridge Jn	33A
HAYDONS ROAD	4, 21A
HAYES	4
HAYWARDS HEATH	15C
HEADCORN	10C
HEATHROW TERMINALS 1,2,3	43C
HEATHROW TERMINAL 4	43C
HEDGE END	28A
HENDON CENTRAL	39A
HERMITAGE, THE	34E
HERNE BAY	9A
HERNE HILL	4
HERON QUAYS	47
HERSHAM	21B
HERSTON	35E
HEVER	14B
Heywood Road Jn	33A
HIGH BARNET	39A
HIGH BROOMS	18A
HIGH ROCKS	14B
HIGH STREET KENSINGTON	44A, 44B
HIGHAM	7
HIGHBURY & ISLINGTON	40C
HIGHGATE	39A
HILDENBOROUGH	6B
HILLINGDON	42A
HILSEA	26C
HINCHLEY WOOD	21B, 22
HINTON ADMIRAL	31A
HITHER GREEN	3B, 5
HOLBORN	37C, 46A
HOLLAND PARK	37B
HOLLINGBOURNE	11A
HOLLOWAY ROAD	46A
HOLMWOOD	19A
HOLTON HEATH	31B
HONITON	34B
HONOR OAK PARK	4
HOO JUNCTION	7
HOOK	24C
HORLEY	15B
HORNCHURCH	45B
HORSHAM	19B
HORSLEY	23
HORSTED KEYNES	35D
Hothfield	11A
HOUNSLOW	1A
HOUNSLOW CENTRAL	43C
HOUNSLOW EAST	43C
HOUNSLOW WEST	43C
HOVE	16, 20A
HURST GREEN	14B
HYDE PARK CORNER	46A

HYTHE	18E
Hythe (Hants)	30A
ICKENHAM	42A
IFIELD	19B
ISLAND GARDENS	47
ISLE OF WIGHT STEAM RLY	35C
ISLEWORTH	1A
JEFFERSTONE LANE	18E
JUBILEE LINE	42, 43A
KEARSNEY	13
KEMPTON PARK	21B
KEMSING	7
KEMSLEY	8B
KEMSLEY DOWN	8C
KENLEY	14C
KENNINGTON	39B
KENSAL GREEN	41A
KENSINGTON OLYMPIA	1A, 44A
KENT & EAST SUSSEX RAILWAY	13A
KENT HOUSE	4
KENTISH TOWN	39A
KENTON	41A
KEW BRIDGE	1A
KEW GARDENS	1A
KIDBROOKE	5
KILBURN	42B
KILBURN PARK	41B
KINGS CROSS ST. PANCRAS	39B, 40C,
	44B, 46A
KINGS CROSS THAMESLINK	44B
KINGSBURY	42A
KINGSCOTE	35D
Kingsnorth	7
KINGSTON	21B
KINGSWOOD	14C
KNIGHTSBRIDGE	46A
KNOCKHOLT	6A
LADBROKE GROVE	44B
LADYWELL	3A, 4
LAKE	35C
LAMBETH NORTH	41B
LANCASTER GATE	37C
LANCING	20A
LATIMER ROAD	44B
Laverstock Jns	32B
LEATHERHEAD	22
LEE	5
LEICESTER SQUARE	39B, 46A
LEIGH	10B
LENHAM	11A
LES FONTINETTES	12D
LEWES	16
LEWISHAM	3A, 4, 5
LEYTON	38A
LEYTONSTONE	38A
Lillie Bridge Depot	44A
LIMEHOUSE	47
LINGFIELD	14B
LIPHOOK	26B
LISS	26B
LITTLEHAMPTON	20C
LITTLEHAVEN	19B
LIVERPOOL STREET	37C, 44B, 46C
LONDON BRIDGE	3A, 39B, 43A
LONDON CANNON STREET	3A
LONDON CHARING CROSS	3A
LONDON KENSINGTON OLYMPIA	1A, 44A
LONDON ROAD (Brighton)	16
LONDON ROAD (Guildford)	23
London Road Depot	41B
LONDON VICTORIA	2
LONDON WATERLOO	2
LONGCROSS	25A
LONGFIELD	7
Lords	43A
LOUGHBOROUGH JUNCTION	3A, 4
Lovers Walk	16
LOWER SYDENHAM	4
Ludgershall	32A
Lullingstone	6A, 7
Lydd Town	18D
LYMINGTON PIER	30B
LYMINGTON TOWN	30B
LYMPSTONE COMMANDO	34B
LYMPSTONE VILLAGE	34B
LYNDHURST ROAD	30A
MAIDA VALE	41B
MAIDEN NEWTON	35A
MAIDSTONE BARRACKS	7
MAIDSTONE EAST	7
MAIDSTONE WEST	7
MALDEN MANOR	22
MANOR HOUSE	46A
MANSION HOUSE	44B
MARBLE ARCH	37C
Marchwood	30A
MARDEN	10C
MARGATE	9A
MARINA (BLACK ROCK)	16
Maritime Freightliner Terminal	30A
Marlborough Road	43A
MARTINS MILL	13
MARTIN'S HERON	25B
MARYLEBONE	41B
MAZE HILL	3A
MESTEAD & FOUR MARKS	24D
MEOPHAM	7
MERSTHAM	15A
MERTON PARK	22
METROPOLITAN LINE	41C, 42, 44B
MICHELDEVER	27C
MID-HANTS RAILWAY	24D
MILE END	37C, 45A
MILFORD	26A
MILL HILL EAST	39A
MILLBROOK	29
MINSTER	9A

MITCHAM	22
MITCHAM JUNCTION	22
Monkton & Carne	31D
MONUMENT	44B
MOORGATE	39B, 44B
MOOR PARK	42A
MORDEN	40A
MORDEN ROAD	22
MORDEN SOUTH	22
MORETON	31C
MORNINGTON CRESCENT	39B
MORTIMER	27A
MORTLAKE	1A
MOTSPUR PARK	22
MOTTINGHAM	5
MOULSECOOMB	16
MOUNT PLEASANT	46C
Mountfield	18B
MUDCHUTE	47
NEASDEN	42B
Neasden Depot	42B
Neasden Freight Terminal	1A
NETLEY	29
NEW BECKENHAM	4
NEW CROSS	3A, 45C
New Cross Depot	45C
NEW CROSS GATE	3A, 45C
NEW ELTHAM	5
NEW HYTHE	7
NEW MALDEN	20A, 20B, 22
NEW MILTON	31A
NEW ROMNEY	18E
New Wandsworth	4
NEWBURY PARK	38A
NEWHAVEN HARBOUR	17A
NEWHAVEN MARINE	17A
NEWHAVEN TOWN	17A
NEWINGTON	8A
NORBITON	21B
NORBURY	4
NORDEN	35E
NORMANS BAY	17B
NORTH ACTON	37B
NORTH CAMP	24C
NORTH DULWICH	4
NORTH EALING	43B
NORTH GREENWICH	43A
NORTH HARROW	42A
North Pole International Depot	1A
NORTH SHEEN	1A
North Weald	38B
North Wembley	41A
NORTHERN LINE	39, 40
NORTHFIELDS	43B
NORTHFLEET	7
NORTHIAM	13A
NORTHOLT	37A
Northumberland Park Depot	40C
NORTHWICK PARK	42A
NORTHWOOD	42A
NORTHWOOD HILLS	42A
NORWOOD JUNCTION	4, 14C
NOTTING HILL GATE	37B, 44B
NUNHEAD	3A, 4
NUTBOURNE	20D
NUTFIELD	10A, 15A
OAKWOOD	46B
OCKLEY	19A
OLD STREET	39B
Ongar	38B
ORE	18C
ORPINGTON	6A
OSTERLEY	43C
Osterley & Spring Grove	43C
OTFORD	6A, 7
OVAL	40A
OVERTON	27B
OXFORD CIRCUS	37C, 40B, 41B
OXSHOTT	22
OXTED	14B
PADDINGTON	41B, 44B
PADDINGTON	46C
PADDOCK WOOD	10C
PARK LANE	36D
PARK ROYAL	43B
PARKSTONE	31A, 31B
PARSONS GREEN	44A
PASTON PLACE	16
Paulsgrove	26C
PECKHAM RYE	3A, 4
PENGE EAST	4
PENGE WEST	4
PENSHURST	10B
PERIVALE	37B
PETERSFIELD	26B
PETTS WOOD	6A
PEVENSEY BAY	17B
PEVENSEY & WESTHAM	17A
PICCADILLY CIRCUS	41B, 46A
PICCADILLY LINE	43B, 43C, 44A, 46A, 46B
PIMLICO	40B
PINESWAY JUNCTION	36D
PINHOE	34B
PINNER	42A
Pirbright Jn	23
PLAISTOW	45A
PLUCKLEY	10D
PLUMPTON	15C
PLUMSTEAD	5
POKESDOWN	31A
POLEGATE	17A
POLSLOE BRIDGE	34B
POOLE	31B
POPLAR	47
PORTCHESTER	26C
PORTSLADE	20A
PORTSMOUTH & SOUTHSEA	26C
PORTSMOUTH HARBOUR	26C
POST OFFICE RAILWAY	46C

PRESTON PARK 16
PRESTON ROAD 42A
PRINCE REGENT 47
Pudding Mill Lane 47
PULBOROUGH 19C
PURLEY 14C
PURLEY OAKS 14C
PUTNEY 1A
PUTNEY BRIDGE 44A

QUEENBOROUGH 8B
QUEENS PARK 41B
QUEENSBURY 42A
QUEENSTOWN RD (Battersea) 2
QUEENSWAY 37B
Quidhampton 32B

RAINHAM 8A
RAMSGATE 9A
RAVENSBOURNE 4
RAVENSCOURT PARK 44A
RAYNERS LANE 42A
RAYNES PARK 21A, 22
READING 27A
READING WEST 27A
REDBRIDGE (BR) 30A
REDBRIDGE (LU) 38A
REDHILL 15A
REEDHAM 14C
REGENT'S PARK 41B
REIGATE 15A
REUNION 18E
RICHMOND 1A
RICKMANSWORTH 41C
RIDDLESDOWN 14C
Ridham Dock 8B
ROBERTSBRIDGE 18B
ROCHESTER 7
RODING VALLEY 38A
ROLVENDEN 13A
ROMNEY SANDS 18E
ROMSEY 32C
ROPLEY 24D
ROTHERHITHE 45C
ROWLANDS CASTLE 26B
ROYAL ALBERT 47
ROYAL OAK 44B
ROYAL VICTORIA 47
RUISLIP 42A
Ruislip Depot 37A
RUISLIP GARDENS 37A
RUISLIP MANOR 42A
RUSSELL SQUARE 46A
RYDE ESPLANADE 35C
RYDE PIER HEAD 35C
RYDE ST. JOHNS RD 35C
RYE 18D

ST. DENYS 29
ST. HELIER 22
ST. JAMES PARK 34C
ST. JAMES'S PARK 44B
ST. JOHNS 3A, 4
ST. JOHNS WOOD 43A
ST. LEONARDS WARRIOR SQUARE 18C
St. Leonards West Marina 17B
ST. MARGARETS 1A
ST. MARY CRAY 6A
St. Mary's 44B
ST. PAUL'S 37C
SALFORDS 15A
SALISBURY 32B
SANDERSTEAD 14C
SANDHURST 25B
SANDLING 11C
SANDOWN 35C
SANDWICH 9A
SEAFORD 17A
SEATON 34D
Seaton Junction 34A
SEATON TRAMWAY 34D
SELHURST 4, 14C
Selhurst Depot 14C
SELLING 8B
Selsdon 14C
Semley 33B
SEVEN SISTERS 40C
SEVENOAKS 6A
Sevington Sidings 11B
SHADWELL 45C, 47
SHAKESPEARE STAFF HALT 13
SHALFORD 24A
SHANKLIN 35C
SHAWFORD 27C
SHEERNESS-ON-SEA 8B
SHEFFIELD PARK 35D
SHEPHERDS BUSH 37B, 44A
SHEPHERDSWELL 13
SHEPPERTON 21B
SHERBORNE 33C
SHOLING 29
SHOREDITCH 45C
SHOREHAM 6A, 7
SHOREHAM-BY-SEA 20A
SHORTLANDS 4, 6A
SIDCUP 5
SITTINGBOURNE 8B, 8C
SITTINGBOURNE & KEMSLEY LIGHT RLY 8C
SLADE GREEN 5
SLOANE SQUARE 44B
SMALLBROOK JUNCTION 35C
SMITHAM 14C
SNARESBROOK 38A
SNODLAND 7
SNOWDOWN 13
SOLE STREET 7
SOUTH ACTON 1A
SOUTH CROYDON 14C
SOUTH EALING 43B
SOUTH HARROW 43B
SOUTH KENSINGTON 44B, 46A
South Kentish Town 39A

SOUTH KENTON 41A
SOUTH MERTON 22
SOUTH QUAY 47
SOUTH RUISLIP 37A
SOUTH WIMBLEDON (Merton) 40A
SOUTH WOODFORD 38A
SOUTHAMPTON AIRPORT PARKWAY 29
SOUTHAMPTON CENTRAL 29
Southampton Eastern Docks 29
Southampton Western Docks 29
SOUTHBOURNE 20D
SOUTHEASE 17A
Southerham Jn 17A
SOUTHFIELDS 44A
SOUTHGATE 46B
SOUTHWARK 43A
SOUTHWICK 20A
STAINES 25A
STAMFORD BROOK 44A
STANMORE 42A
STAPLEHURST 10C
STEPNEY GREEN 45A
Stewarts Lane 2
STOCKWELL 40A, 40B
STONE CROSSING 7
STONEBRIDGE PARK 1A, 1B, 41A
STONEGATE 18A
STONELEIGH 22
STRATFORD 37C, 43A, 47
STRAWBERRY HILL 1A, 21B
STREATHAM 4
STREATHAM COMMON 4
STREATHAM HILL 4
STROOD 7
STURRY 9B
SUDBURY HILL 43B
SUDBURY TOWN 43B
SUNBURY 21B
SUNDRIDGE PARK 3B
SUNNINGDALE 25A
SUNNYMEADS 25A
SURBITON 21B, 22
SURREY QUAYS 45C
SUTTON 22
SUTTON COMMON 22
SWALE 8B
SWANAGE 35E
SWANAGE RAILWAY 35E
SWANLEY 6A, 7
SWANSCOMBE 7
SWANWICK 26C
SWAY 30B
SWAYTHLING 29
SWISS COTTAGE 43A
SYDENHAM 4
SYDENHAM HILL 4
SYON LANE 1A

TADWORTH 14C
TATTENHAM CORNER 14C
TEDDINGTON 21B
TEMPLE 44B
TEMPLECOMBE 33C
TENTERDEN TOWN 13A
TEYNHAM 8B
Thamesport 7
THEYDON BOIS 38B
THORNFORD 35A
THORNTON HEATH 4
THREE BRIDGES 15B, 19B
THREE OAKS 18C
Tilmanstone 13
Tinsley Green 15B
TISBURY 33B
TOLWORTH 22
TONBRIDGE 10B
TOOTING 4
TOOTING BEC 40A
TOOTING BROADWAY 40A
TOPSHAM 34B
TOTTENHAM COURT ROAD 37C, 39B
TOTTENHAM HALE 40C
TOTTERIDGE & WHETSTONE 39A
TOTTON 30A
TOWER GATEWAY 47
TOWER HILL 44B
TUFNELL PARK 39A
TULSE HILL 4
TUNBRIDGE WELLS 18A
TUNBRIDGE WELLS WEST 14B
TUNBRIDGE WELLS & ERIDGE RLY 14B
TURNHAM GREEN 44A
TURNPIKE LANE 46B
TWICKENHAM 1A

UCKFIELD 14A
UPMINSTER 45B
UPMINSTER BRIDGE 45B
UPNEY 45A
UPPER HALLIFORD 21B
UPPER WARLINGHAM 14C
UPTON PARK 45C
UPWEY 31D
UXBRIDGE 42A

VAUXHALL 2, 40B
VICTORIA 2, 40B, 44B
VICTORIA LINE 40B, 40C
VIRGINIA WATER 25A
VOLKS ELECTRIC RAILWAY 16

WADDON 22
WADDON MARSH 22
WADHURST 18A
Wallers Ash 27C
WALLINGTON 22
WALMER 13
WALTHAMSTOW CENTRAL 40C
WALTON-ON-THAMES 21B
WANBOROUGH 23
WANDSWORTH COMMON 4

WANDSWORTH ROAD 2
WANDSWORTH TOWN 1A
WANSTEAD 38A
WAPPING 45C
WARBLINGTON 20D
WAREHAM 31C
WARMINSTER 33A
WARNHAM 19A
WARREN 13
WARREN STREET 39B, 40B, 40C
WARWICK AVENUE 41B
WATERINGBURY 13A
WATERLOO 2, 38C, 39B, 41B, 43A
WATERLOO EAST 3A
WATERLOO & CITY LINE 38C
WATFORD 41C
WELLING 5
WEMBLEY CENTRAL 1B, 41A
Wembley European Freight 1B
Wembley Intercity Depot 1B
WEMBLEY PARK 42B
WEST ACTON 37B
WEST BROMPTON 44A
WEST BYFLEET 21B, 23
WEST CROYDON 14C, 22
WEST DULWICH 4
WEST FINCHLEY 39A
WEST HAM 43A, 45A
WEST HAMPSTEAD 42B, 43A
WEST HARROW 42A
WEST INDIA QUAY 47
WEST KENSINGTON 44A
WEST MALLING 7
WEST NORWOOD 4
WEST RUISLIP 37A
WEST ST. LEONARDS 18C
WEST SUTTON 22
WEST WICKHAM 4
WEST WORTHING 20B
WESTBOURNE PARK 44B
WESTBURY 33A
WESTCOMBE PARK 3A
WESTENHANGER 11B
WESTERN DISTRICT OFFICE 46C
WESTFERRY 47
WESTGATE-ON-SEA 9A
WESTMINSTER 43A, 44B
WEYBRIDGE 21B
WEYMOUTH 31D
WEYMOUTH QUAY 31D
WHIMPLE 34B
WHITCHURCH 32A
WHITE CITY 37B
WHITECHAPEL 44B, 45C
WHITSTABLE 9A
WHITTON 1A
WHYTELEAFE 14C
WHYTELEAFE SOUTH 14C
Willesborough Sidings 11B
Willesden Brent Sidings 1A
WILLESDEN GREEN 42B
WILLESDEN JUNCTION 1A, 41A
Wilton 32B, 33B
WIMBLEDON 21A, 22
WIMBLEDON CHASE 21A, 22
WIMBLEDON PARK 21A, 44A
Wimbledon Traincare Depot 21A
WINCHELSEA: 18C
WINCHESTER 27C
WINCHFIELD 24C
WINDSOR & ETON RIVERSIDE 25A
Winfrith 31C
WINNERSH 25B
WINNERSH TRIANGLE 25B
WITLEY 26A
WITTERSHAM ROAD 13A
WIVELSFIELD 15C
WOKING 23
WOKINGHAM 25B
WOLDINGHAM 14C
WOOD GREEN 46B
WOODFORD 38A
WOODMANSTERNE 14C
WOODSIDE 4
WOODSIDE PARK 39A
WOOL 31C
WOOLSTON 29
WOOLWICH ARSENAL 5
WOOLWICH DOCKYARD 5
WOOTTON 35C
WORCESTER PARK 22
Worgret Jn 31C
WORPLESDON 23
WORTHING 20B
Worting Jn 27B
WRAYSBURY 24A
WYE 11B

YALDING 10C
YEOVIL JUNCTION 33D
YEOVIL PEN MILL 35B
YETMINSTER 35A
York Road 46A

ENGINEER'S LINE REFERENCES

ELR	ROUTE DESCRIPTION
AAV	Ascot Jn - Ash Vale Jn
ACR	Ashford 'E' Jn-Canterbury West - Ramsgate
ACW	Acton Canal Wharf - Willesden
AGW	Angerstein Jn - Angerstein Wharf
AHG	Nine Elms Jn - Linford Street Jn
AJB	Addlestone Jn - Byfleet Jn
ANL	Acton and Northolt line (via Greenford East)
APL	Appledore Jn - Lydd Town - Dungeness
ATG	Turnham Green (LU Bdy) - Gunnersbury Jn
ATH	Ashford 'D' Jn - Hastings
ATL	Peckham Rye - Battersea Park Jn (Atlantic line/South London line)
AWL	Acton East - Acton Wells Jn
BAE	Basingstoke (Worting Jn) - Exeter St. Davids
BAY	Bricklayers Arms Branch
BBD	Bournemouth West Carriage Sidings
BBJ	Balham Jn - Beckenham Jn
BBR	Burnham Jn - Bognor Regis
BDH	Brent Curve Jn - Dudding Hill Jn
BEX	St. Johns Jn - Crayford Creek Jn via Bexleyheath
BHL	Berks and Hants line (Southcote Jn - Patney & Westbury Jn)
BJN	Bromley Jn - Norwood Jn
BKE	Basingstoke Branch (Reading Westbury line Jn - Basingstoke)
BLI	Brighton (West Coast) - Littlehampton
BLP	Brockenhurst - Lymington Pier
BME	Buckland Jn - Minster East Jn
BMJ	Blackfriars Jn - Metropolitan Jn
BML	Waterloo (Main lines) - Weymouth (Bournemouth Main line)
BNG	Bromley North - Grove Park Jn
BOK	Broad Street - Old Kew Jn via Hampstead Heath (North London line)
BPJ	Lovers Walk Depot
BSF	Battersea Pier Jn (LCD) - Stewarts Lane - Factory Jn
BSP	Battersea Pier Jn (LBSC) - Stewarts Lane - Longhedge Jn - Pouparts Jn
BTC	Blackheath - Charlton Jn
BTH	South Bermondsey Jn - Sutton - Epsom - Horsham Jn
BTL	Brighton (East Coast) - Lewes Jn
CAT	Brixton Jn - Catford - Shortlands Jn (Catford Loop)
CAW	Cricklewood Curve Jn - Acton Wells Jn
CBM	Cannon Street - Borough Market Jn
CCL	Castle Cary and Langport line
CJA	Copyhold Jn - Ardingly
CJL	Clapham Jn (Ludgate Jn) - Latchmere No.2 Jn
CKL	Longhedge Jn (Calvert Rd Jn) - Latchmere No.1 Jn
CLA	Chart Leacon, Ashford, Depot
CLJ	Clapham Junction Sidings
CMJ	West Croydon - Mitcham (South) Jn
CRA	Crayford Spur 'B' Jn - Crayford Spur 'A' Jn
CSM	Chislehurst Jn - St. Mary Cray Jn (Chatham Loops)
CSW	Metropolitan Jn - Cannon Street South Jn
CWJ	Camden Jn - Watford Jn (DC Electric lines)
CYD	Gillingham (Kent) - Chatham Dockyard
DAC	Exeter and Devonport line (via Okehampton) (Devon and Cornwall)
DFD	Dover Ferry Dock Jn - Dover Old Train Ferry Dock
ECR	Eastleigh East Jn - (Chandler's Ford) - Romsey Jn
EEA	Elmers End Jn - Addiscombe
EKR	Shepherdswell Jn - Tilmanstone Cly (EKLR)
EMT	Exmouth Jn - Exmouth
ERY	Exeter Riverside Yard
ETF	Eastleigh West Jn - Fareham East Jn
EYD	Eastleigh Yards etc
FDM	Faversham - Dover Marine Jn
FFH	Folkestone East Jn - Folkestone Harbour
FJJ	Farlington Jn - Cosham Jn
FJL	Ford Jn - Littlehampton Jn
FLL	Factory Jn - Longhedge Jn - Lavender Hill Jn - Clapham Jn (Ludgate Jn)
FSS	Fenchurch Street - Shoeburyness
FTB	Fareham West Jn - Bedenham Sidings
FTL	Farringdon Jn - (Ludgate) Blackfriars
FUR	Worgret Jn - Furzebrook Sidings
GTW	Guildford North Jn - Wokingham Jn
HAG	Hamworthy Jn - Hamworthy Goods
HAM	Surbiton (Down Hampton Court Line Jn) - Hampton Court
HDR	Hither Green Jn - Dartford - Rochester Bridge Jn
HGG	Hurst Green Jn - East Grinstead
HGP	Hither Green/Grove Park sidings
HHH	(Holborn Viaduct) Blackfriars - Herne Hill South Jn
HHT	Herne Hill South Jn - Tulse Hill Jn
HJW	Hounslow Jn - Whitton Jn
HOU	Barnes Jn - Hounslow - Feltham Jn (Hounslow loop)
HSE	Hawkesbury Street Jn - Archcliffe Jn
HTG	Hoo Jn - Grain
IOW	Ryde Pier Head - Shanklin (Isle of Wight)
KGC	Kensal Green Jn - Willesden (City lines)
KJE	Keymer Jn - Eastbourne
LAV	Laverstock North Jn - Laverstock South Jn
LBC	London Bridge (Platforms 14-16) - Bricklayers Arms Jn (South London line)
LBW	London Bridge (Platforms 8-13) - Windmill Bridge Jn
LCH	Lewisham East Jn (Ladywell line) - Hayes
LEC	London, Euston - Crewe
LEE	Lee Jn - Lee Spur Jn
LEJ	Leatherhead Jn - Effingham Jn
LLG	Willesden, West London Jn - Sudbury Jn (Low Level Goods)
LLL	Parks Bridge Jn - Ladywell Jn (Ladywell Loop)
LOC	Loughborough In - Canterbury Road Jn
LTC	Loughborough Jn - Cambria Jn
LTH	Leigham Jn - Tulse Hill Jn (Leigham Spur)
LUD	Andover Jn - Ludgershall
LVT	Lewisham Vale Jn - Tanners Hill Jn
MCJ	Marylebone - Claydon LNE Jn via Harrow-on-the-Hill
MCL	Kentish Town Jn - Moorgate (Midland City line)
MIS	Millbrook - Southampton Western Docks
MJW	Mitcham (North) Junction - Wimbledon, Mitcham Line Jn
MLN	Paddington - Bristol - Penzance ('Main Line')
MOD	Dinton East Jn - Chilmark Sidings
MPC	Motspur Park - Chessington South
MSW	Minster South Jn - Minster West Jn
NAJ	Neasden South Jn - Aynho Jn
NBB	New Beckenham Jn - Beckenham Jn
NCS	Courthill Loop Jn North - Courthill Loop Jn South (Courthill Loop)
NFE	Norwood Jn (Wallington Line Jn) - Epsom Downs
NGL	Hampton Court Jn - Guildford, New Line Jn (New Guildford Line)
NHB	Newhaven Harbour Jn - Newhaven Harbour
NJN	Neasden Curve
NKE	New Kew Jn - Kew East Jn
NKL	North Kent East Jn - Greenwich - Dartford Jn
NMS	New Malden Jn - Shepperton
NSA	Aldershot South Jn - Aldershot North Jn
NTL	Nunhead Jn - Lewisham Jn
NYD	Norwood Yard and Selhurst Workshop Sidings
OJS	Otford Jn - Sevenoaks Jn
PAA	Pirbright Jn - Alton
PAS	Portsmouth, Blackfriars Jn - Portsmouth & Southsea Low Level
PAT	Purley - Caterham
PBE	Putney Bridge (former LU Bdy) - East Putney Jn
PPH	Preston Park - Hove
PPW	Point Pleasant Jn - Wimbledon (LU platforms)
PSF	Perry Street Fork Jn - Slade Green Jn
PWS	Paddock Wood - Strood
RDG	Waterloo (Windsor lines) - Reading
RED	Stoats Nest Jn - Redhill - Earlswood Jn (Redhill line)
RNJ	Reading Spur Jn - Reading New Jn
RPE	Raynes Park Jn - Epsom Jn
RSJ	Redhill, Guildford Line Jn - Shalford Jn
RTJ	Redbridge Jn - Salisbury, Tunnel Jn
RTT	Redhill, Tonbridge Line Jn - Tonbridge West Jn
RWC	Reading West Curve
SAL	Westbury South Jn - Wilton Jn (Salisbury Branch)
SAR	South Acton Jn - Richmond
SBJ	Swanley Jn - Ashford 'B' Jn via Maidstone East
SCC	West London Jn - Latchmere No.3 Junction (Sheepcote Curve)
SCP	Sydenham Jn - Crystal Palace, Tunnel Jn
SCU	South Croydon Jn - Uckfield
SDP	St Denys Jn - Portcreek Jn
SEJ	Sittingbourne, Eastern Jn - Sheerness
SHF	Strawberry Hill Jn - Fulwell Jn
SLC	Stewarts Lane sidings
SLJ	Streatham North Jn (Slow lines) - Streatham South Jn (Slow lines)
SLT	Stonebridge Park - LU Depot
SMS	Streatham South Jn - Sutton, Wimbledon Line or West Jn (via Wimbledon)
SNS	Streatham North Jn (Fast line) - Streatham South Jn (Fast line)
SOY	Northam Jn - Southampton Eastern Docks
SSC	Streatham Jn - Streatham Common Jn
STA	Staines Branch
STS	Southerham Jn - Seaford
SWE	Staines Jn - Windsor & Eton Riverside
SWY	Stert and Westbury line, Patney and Chirton - Westbury
TAT	Purley (Chipstead Line) Jn - Tattenham Corner
TBH	Three Bridges Jn - Havant Jn via Horsham
TLP	Bickley Jn - Petts Wood Jn (Tonbridge Loops)
TML	Saltwood Jn/Continental Jn - Eurotunnel boundary (Trans-Manche Link)
TSJ	Twickenham Jn - Shacklegate Jn
TTF	Totton - Fawley
TTH	Tonbridge East Jn - Hastings
UHL	Wembley Yard - Willesden (Up High Level Arrival Line)
USY	Up Sidings Yard, Westbury
VIR	Victoria (Eastern) - Ramsgate via Herne Hill and Chatham
VTB	Victoria (Central) - Brighton via Streatham Common and Quarry Line
VWW	Virginia Water - Weybridge
WAW	Willesden, Low Level Goods Jn - Acton Wells Jn
WCL	Willesden - Willesden Carriage Shed North via Carriage Lines
WCS	Selhurst Jn - Gloucester Road Jn
WDS	Woodside - Selsdon
WES	Westbury Avoiding line
WEY	Thingley Jn - Dorchester Jn (Weymouth line)
WGS	Willesden Inter City Depot
WJB	Willingdon Jn - Bopeep Jn
WKG	Woking Yards
WLL	Clapham Jn, Falcon Jn - Willesden, West London Jn (West London Line)
WMB	Willesden HL Jn - Mitre Bridge Jn
WMS	Sittingbourne Western Jn - Middle Jn
WPH	Woking Jn - Portsmouth Harbour (Portsmouth Direct Line)
WPK	Wimbledon Park and Depot Sidings
WTH	West Norwood Jn - Tulse Hill Jn (West Norwood Spur)
WTQ	Weymouth Jn - Weymouth Quay
WTS	Willesden Through Sdgs - Harlesden to Brent
WYL	Westbury East Loop
WZS	Willesden Traction Maintenance Depot Sdgs
XTD	Charing Cross - Dover Western Docks via Chelsfield
YJP	Yeovil Pen Mill Jn - Yeovil Jn